SANDBOX SCIENTIST

Real Science Activities For Little Kids

Michael E. Ross
Illustrated by Mary Anne Lloyd

CHICAGO

PRESS

Library of Congress Cataloging-in-Publication Data

Ross, Michael Elsohn, 1952–

    Sandbox scientist : real science activities for little kids /
Michael E. Ross

      p. cm.

    Includes bibliographical references

    Summary: A guide for adults in setting up activities for children
ages two to eight to discover scientific facts about water, matter, air,
light, etc., using familiar materials.

    ISBN 1-55652-248-7 (pbk.)

    1. Science—Experiments—Juvenile literature. [1. Science—
Experiments. 2. Experiments.] I. Title.

Q164.R68 1995

372.3'5044—dc20   95-13508

                                                    CIP

                                                     AC

The author and the publisher disclaim all liability incurred in
connection with the use of the information contained in this book.

Published by Chicago Review Press, Incorporated

814 N. Franklin Street, Chicago, Illinois 60610

ISBN 1-55652-248-7

Printed in the United States of America

For my parents, Bill and Jeanne Ross, for encouraging exploration and for my son, Nick, for sharing his wonder

Contents

Foreword

Like scientists, children make their discoveries through creative activity. They do not record just what they see. They experiment. This basic principle has been transformed into the developmentally appropriate practice approach and constructivism as recommended by the National Association for the Education of Young Children.

This book, *Sandbox Scientist*, is a major contribution to the field of early childhood education because it provides practices and activities that reflect the best thinking of the early childhood profession. Michael Ross now adds "Wondering is one of the professional missions of childhood. Life is far richer when we accept the wonder of kids. As kids explore, they bump into the boundaries of big ideas."

The materials and activities presented in this book are familiar to most of us. They are indeed child centered. The author shows how the experience that comes from the activities is more important than the activity itself. Some teachers will be shocked to learn that hands-on science alone can be boring and destructive. The point is that activities must be presented from a constructivist perspective, which acknowledges that children and adults need to form their own hypotheses and keep trying them out through mental action, physical manipulations, and social interaction. In young children this process most often resembles what we call play.

The sensitivity with which the author describes the activities in this book aptly exemplifies the process of the cycle of learning, from awareness and exploration to inquiry and utilization for meaningful learning to take place. In each of the opportunities for learning offered in *Sandbox Scientist*, it is easy to imagine how the stages of learning could happen for any child in a natural and growth-producing way.

This book is special because it describes scads of topics related to science, explains the events from a scientific point of view, tells how to set up the activities, relates actual anecdotes that the author observed as children interacted with the scientific experiences. This remarkable and unique assemblage of information represents several years of Michael Ross's real-life data collection, particularly his countless hours of dedicated "kid watching."

Children, teachers, and parents can be grateful for this valuable presentation of how to practice good pedagogy. Furthermore, the extensive annotated reading lists that close each chapter and the resources in the appendix are truly priceless.

Doris O. Smith, Professor Emeriti
Early Childhood Education
California State University, Fresno

Acknowledgments

Thanks to Sherry Grazda and her students in Mckinleyville for inviting me to explore with them. Many thanks to Ellen Jones and Cyndi Rose for always welcoming me and my stuff at the El Portal Child Development Center. I am especially indebted to Allison Bown, who became a true partner in exploring the world of scientists at play. Last, but not least, this book is a tribute to all of the children I watched playing at the El Portal Elementary School, the El Portal Child development Center, and my local neighborhood.

Introduction

Kids are scientists at play. Watch them. While they bake mud pies or construct worm playgrounds, you might catch them conducting playful experiments. Listen to them. Amidst the giggling, you may hear an exchange of astute observations or sensible theories. Playfully explore with them, and you may be astonished at how their attention span far outlasts yours. Children use many of the same science process skills as adult scientists. Similarly, they develop ideas about our world based on experiences with real things. Though kids' naive notions may often seem silly, they are the offspring of serious thought.

Kid science reaches into two worlds, reality and fantasy. As children immerse themselves in rich experiences, the two worlds become more separate. Through experimentation and constant comparison, reality is gently unmasked. Adult "science facts" and prescribed step-by-step experiments are an inadequate substitute for explorations of a child's own choosing. For kid science is divergent rather than linear. It is process rather than product (facts and concepts). It is real science.

Whether you are a parent, teacher, or another caretaker of young children, you can easily become a patron of kid science. All you have to do is let kids explore their world and accumulate a diverse collection of experiences. *Sandbox Scientist* is a guide to outfitting young adventurers for playful expeditions at home, school, or at childcare centers. Included are ideas on how to set up environments that stimulate opened-ended investigations, information on where to get inexpensive or free materials, and tips on recognizing and nurturing science process skills.

Sandbox Scientist is a guide, not a cookbook. Rather than recipes for "Gee whiz, Dr. Science–type experiments," you'll discover ideas, information, and resources to help you assist kids in their own playful science journeys. The science activities consist of putting together and using Explorer Kits. Gather up the recommended materials and whatever additional things you think will spark the kids, and let the learning happen. Put kids with the kits in this book, and scientific exploration will follow.

Explorer Kits

To turn your home or classroom into an exploratorium, all you need is a variety of materials and tools. I have learned to count on kids being interested in most anything if they can explore it in their own way. The array of tools and stuff will often suggest explorations. A child provided with

water and water droppers will likely investigate water drops. A magnifying lens will guide kids toward little things or textures. Play with the materials yourself and see where they lead you!

An Explorer Kit contains an array of tools and materials that sends kids off on various paths of playful investigation. Each kit focuses the kids on a general realm of discovery, but, as you will see, children will choose their own routes. Kits can and should be modified to fit children's reactions and the materials at hand. Allow children to add to and modify the kits. Let it become theirs.

Each Explorer Kit is presented in the following format.

Each one begins with a preview of the basic types of activities kids may engage in, but remember these are open-ended ventures. Very likely, your kids will do something with the materials that no one else in the universe has ever considered doing.

Materials The kit materials are the toys that will guide each new exploration. The lists can and should be modified. Be flexible. Use what you have or what is easy to procure. Encourage kids to contribute materials. Your only major concerns should be the safety of kids and instruments. The diversity and quantity of materials will influence the type of explorations kids embark on.

The Setup Ideas for setting up activities are provided here. Included are suggestions for how to minimize messes and avoid disasters.

The Science As kids explore, they bump into the boundaries of big ideas. An understanding of complex concepts will one day emerge from these experiences. Listed in this section are some of the concepts that may rise out of the experiential mist. If you are a teacher and need to justify playful science to questioning parents or administrators, this section will give you some educationese to spout forth. Occasionally included are examples of types of open-ended questions you could ask. At all costs, refrain from interrupting focused kids. Wait until they engage you in verbal inquiry and then ask as a fellow adventurer, not as a know-it-all adult.

Real Life Science The anecdotes in these sections show you what one group of kids did with the materials. The anecdotes are from a variety of settings (from preschool to elementary school to home) and take place over a period of several years. Many of the children appear in a number of anecdotes at various stages of their lives. It was a real thrill to write about children at two years of age and then chronicle their adventures as five-year-olds. The age of the children mentioned in the anecdotes is noted at the beginning.

Age Appropriateness The purpose of this book is to introduce science to small children as young as two years old, although I have watched children as old as eight have the time of their lives with the Explorer Kits. I've indicated the age appropriateness of each kit by noting the youngest age for which it may be suitable. This rating is meant as a general guideline and certainly varies with the children and the settings that they explore in. Be your own judge.

Kid Science Library Children's books, whether they are fiction or nonfiction, can easily enhance children's explorations. A fascinating book or story can lead to child-initiated investigations. A fascinating exploration can lead to an interest in any books dealing with the topics being explored. At the end of each activity chapter you'll find a list of recommended fiction and nonfiction children's books that relate to chapter topics.

Now you can turn right to the activity chapters and embark on your adventures in early childhood science education, but I recommend that you read a bit further. Though you are undoubtedly eager for action, I have some suggestions that should make your road a bit smoother.

Become a Patron of Kid Science

Lewis and Clark may never have made it out the door without the beneficent patronage of Thomas Jefferson. Unlike adult scientists, children will embark on scientific inquiries without fellowships, grants, or other institutional backing. Unfortunately though, kid investigations are often thwarted for lack of patronage. Whether it's an experiment to test if peas float in milk or a "dig" in the flower bed, kids sometimes just end up doing the "right" thing at the wrong time or in the wrong place. On the other hand, a kid scientist with a supportive elder can usually end up doing science where and when it's appreciated.

An art patron doesn't need to be an artist, nor does a patron of science need be a scientist. So it's no big deal if you don't possess a Ph.D. in astrophysics or entomology; all you need is a big degree of interest. Science, like walking, talking, and breathing, is a process that doesn't require instruction, but it does take practice to perfect. A science patron is a facilitator rather than a direct teacher and there is plenty to do. For example, a patron can:

Watch kids to discover how they playfully explore.

Maintain a "hands-off" attitude so kids can explore in peace.

Encourage and celebrate wonder.

Allow children to follow their own paths of inquiry.

Let kids spend time—it's free!

Support science as a social activity.

Provide safe and enriched environments for exploration.

Equip kids with exploration tools.

Make books and other fonts of knowledge accessible.

The Great Sport of Kid Watching

Kid watching is a revolutionary pastime. Most any kid watcher will soon realize that little folks sure seem to know what they want to do and how to do it. In fact, if the watcher observes with science in mind, the revelations will be that much more remarkable. Science is a process that involves many facets. Observing, communicating, sorting, classifying, questioning, predicting, experimenting, analyzing, and problem solving are just a few of the science process skills children may be witnessed using. These are skills that children employ from the very start and the act of using them is an act of science.

Kid watching reaps awareness. One day at my son's preschool, I observed some of the younger children playing outside at the water table. There were a variety of items in the table. The kids had not been given any guidance other than prohibition against water fights. As I watched, I saw the play evolve from scooping and pouring to "let's make soup." Soon, several children were plucking grass from the lawn and "cooking" up a vegetable broth. During this imaginary culinary session, I observed the children sharing ideas, experimenting with materials, analyzing results, and constantly communicating. The teacher who was supervising the kids obviously did not see any of this. She was new to the child development center and was asserting a strong presence. She told the kids to stop picking grass, asked them not to pour water on the ground, and generally disrupted their play. As her intervention continued, the kids slowly drifted away. Unfortunately, she had preconceived notions of what the materials should have been used for.

Later when I discussed this unnecessary meddling with the preschool director, she suggested that I ask the new teacher to observe the kids and take some notes for me. The next day, I made my request and, by the end of the morning, I had a fully converted kid watcher. The new teacher was fascinated by her observations. She realized how much was happening and saw sense in the kids' actions.

Be a Kid Watcher

Watching kids and recording what they do is a very intriguing and practical occupation. By itself, watching is fine, but writing may be necessary to achieve deeper understanding. Writing requires an intense scrutiny of the pace and dimension of kids' play. It reveals children's interests and guides us in facilitating further explorations. When we can anticipate what kids are getting into, it is far easier to provide them with tools and materials to keep them going.

Records of kids' actions and language are useful in themselves. A teacher or caregiver can use notes as an assessment of individual interests, skills, and growth. A parent can store them as memories.

Wonderful Scientists

Imagine relaxing in a soft, flowery meadow watching big puffy clouds and wondering about immense things like far-off galaxies or infinity. Most folks unfortunately don't find much time to wonder, unless, of course, they are kids. Children's minds are full of wonder and that is why they are wonderful scientists. They ponder. They challenge facts. They try to figure it all out. They ask questions all the time. Why? How? What?

Why aren't there purple ants? How does a CD work? What is fire? The questions bubble forth at amazing speed and discontinuity. Questions just appear, and, to the adult compelled by a factoid-oriented education, they are overwhelming. Have you ever found yourself saying or wanting to say, "because, just because"? Most adults are uncomfortable with questions because we were taught not to ask questions that didn't have answers. Teachers and parents drilled us with display questions, such as "When did Columbus sail the ocean blue?" There's only one answer to that question.

No right-minded kid would ever ask questions like that. Very few taught us by saying, "That's a great question, Sally. We can spend a day or week or month pursuing it, if that's what you want to do." No, it didn't take us long to find out that adults were in charge of questions.

Following Wonder

As questioners, kids are dilettantes. A question about space may be followed by a question about dogs and then a question about deodorant. Kids are like space travelers on a mission to find out

everything they can about the planet they've landed on. Whether they really are from a foreign planet we'll have to leave to further consideration, but they definitely are on a mission. Wondering is one of the professional missions of childhood and, as adults, we can do a lot better than to respond with "because." We can go way beyond feeling compelled to have answers. We can go all the way and get caught up in the act of wonderment.

"Why aren't there purple ants?" asks your kid.

"Gee, I never wondered about that before. Are you sure there aren't? Could they be living someplace we've never been to?" you respond. You quit your job, you sell your house, and off you go with your child on an expedition in search of purple ants.

Whether we trip off on little explorations with our children, lead them by the hand to visit the neighbor who knows about bugs, or assault the local librarian with our questions, life is far richer when we accept the wonder of kids. Children will only expect us to be walking encyclopedias if we always have an answer. It's OK to answer with an affirmation: "Wow, I wonder, too." You can even ask another question: "Why aren't there lavender ants?" or "I wonder if we can find a book about ants?" or "Do you think Timmy's mom might know, she's a gardener?" As a big person, you can support exploration by leading children to the resources that they need. If you can do this and give up the role of having to spout answers, "because" may almost never pop out of your mouth.

The Question Book

Answers aren't always worth remembering, but questions are. Kids frequently ask questions that could take a lifetime to follow. Every question is valuable, especially the ones that aren't easy to answer. We can teach children the value of questions even when we don't have the time to help them explore. Recording questions in a special notebook is one way to acknowledge questions without becoming entangled in answering. Collecting questions can lead to discovering kids' interests. It can also become an album of the adventures of youthful curiosity. It's not hard.

Scribble down some of those off-the-wall ponderings. Perhaps you'll find yourself entering some outrageous questions of your own.

The Pathless Way

Real explorers tread their own paths to discovery. Kids do the same thing when they are allowed to explore freely. The more materials, tools, time, and space they are provided, the more divergent their paths may be. Prescriptive science activities confine the breadth and intensity of a child's inquiry. In fact, many young children actively rebel when placed in a situation where there is only one trail to take. When this happens, "hands-on" science can become a nightmare of turned-off kids taking out their frustration on the stuff in front of them. Tools are damaged. Creatures are harmed. "Hands-on" science is delegated to the back burner.

Several years ago when I began testing open-ended science in a k/1 class, three active first-graders served as my gauge to what activities were appropriate. During the previous year, I had observed and taught these boys while developing new primary-grade science activities. Even though the activities were hands-on, none were of the kids' own choosing or design. Though the other children basically stayed in tune with the teacher's instruction, these boys had their own ideas about how to interact with the materials. For example, during one small group session of observing and discussing rolypolies, one of the boys crawled under the table. Instead of discussing rolypolies, he was being a rolypoly.

Later, when I provided them with rolypolies, magnifying lenses, leaves, stems, a watercolor brush, little cups, and no directions, they explored with vigor. The discussion happened, too—like real discussions, with everyone talking when they felt like it. They shared ideas and asked questions. They told jokes and engaged in sessions of "let's pretend." They were free to go when they pleased. No one was hostage to the situation, and those that came back returned because they wanted to be there.

Another time, I brought snails to a k/1/2 class. All of the kids asked for a snail to play with except Maira, a kindergartner. I noticed her on the other side of the room playing with some ramps and marbles that I had brought into class months before. Despite all the snail-inspired commotion, Maira played with her ramps and observed the marbles intimately. She was trying to figure out

something and the snails would just have to wait, which they did. A few days later, it was Maira's time for snails.

Kid Time

"Kids have a short attention span," I was told in education school. What adult who spends time with kids could actually believe this? The kid who can't get ready to go or get home in time for dinner is usually engaged in some fascinating endeavor. He or she may have been focused for hours, yet is still absorbed. To a casual observer it may appear that the child is not doing much, but that is a result of insufficient observation.

Spy on children in a rich environment with many choices of activities, and you will see a wide range of attention. Some kids may be so transfixed that day could pass into night and they might not even notice. Other children may flit from one thing to the next. In time, most will settle into something, but then again they might be just having a flitty type of day. On another day with different circumstances and choices, the kid who usually flits may be engaged in one activity for a long time.

When the children were playing at the water tubs one day, Allison invented a water timer. She placed a yogurt container with a hole poked in the bottom on top of a plastic bottle. Drip. Drip. Drip. Allison watched drops fall into the bottle. After a while, she showed the invention to other children and then to the teacher. Allison wondered how long it would take for the bottle to fill. When recess came, she did not want to go unless she could bring her in-progress experiment. With the teacher's permission, Allison watched her timer through recess and then back in the classroom. Although neither Allison nor any of the other children had a sense of minutes or hours, they were all interested in Allison's watery hourglass. Had she been denied the time to pursue her experiment, she would have perhaps gone one step further in developing a short attention span. She would have gotten the message, no matter how subliminal, that her experiment was not important. Learning takes time.

One first-grade boy that I frequently observed was diagnosed with attention deficit disorder. It was a struggle for him to remain attentive to directed activities, but his attention was boundless when given freedom to experiment and explore. When we played with flying things, this boy experimented through recess. His enthusiasm not only carried him along but spurred other children into deeper and more complex problem solving.

We all learn at different levels of attention, and kids learn best when given choices and the time to explore. Perhaps television and heavily fragmented daily routines create kids with shorter attention spans. As adults leading scheduled lives, it may be difficult to get a sense of kid time, but try. Watch children at play. Daydream about your own play as a child. Live a day without your watch.

Readiness

When the slimy earthworms came to preschool, Claire and Denise, both two-and-a-half-year-olds, kept their distance. Other children petted and played with the worms, but Claire and Denise shrieked and giggled at the periphery. For nearly an hour, they played at being afraid of the worms, but the joyful exploration of the other kids drew them closer and closer. They were cuddling slimy worms the very next day.

I have some friends who keep trying to get me to sky dive. If the opportunity stays open, I may take the leap someday—but, no thanks, not today. We all need the time to take our leaps.

Kids, like most of us, learn best when they are ready to. Trust them to know when the time has come.

A Place for Exploration

Though beaches, woods, parks, and even vacant lots are a kid explorer's paradise, the backyard, schoolyard, or classroom can become equally alluring. All kids need is diversity and surprises. A walk in the park may reveal hidden caterpillars or sparkling rocks. The discoveries are unpredictable. When we supply our kids with a variety of materials and tools, or when we grow gardens or take in small critters as visitors, we are sowing adven-

tures. It doesn't cost much in time or money. It needn't be dangerous or messy. You merely need the time and place.

Once children are immersed in investigations, only personal and material safety should be of concern. While exploring rocks in class one day, three rowdy first-grade boys began pounding rocks together. Not only were rock chips flying, but the table they were working at was suffering abuse. Rather than end their exploration, we merely relocated it and made it more rewarding. Outside on the blacktop, I showed them how they could smash the rocks with a hammer. By placing the rocks inside an old towel, they were safe from flying rock fragments (later we also incorporated safety glasses). The only other safety issue was making sure the kids didn't bonk each other with the hammers, which we solved by drawing chalk circles for the kids to sit in. The boys crushed rocks for over an hour, all the while comparing the hardness, texture, and color of the broken pieces.

Wherever kids go, entropy follows. To an adult, a mess is something that must be cleaned up. To a kid, it is merely a sign that something interesting has happened. When kids explore new materials, a mess is often inevitable. Try to anticipate the type of mess that may occur and then choose the best locale.

Children will maintain an interest in an experiment or new materials for many days, weeks, or even months. If you can store the materials in an accessible place, children will be able to continue explorations when they please. My son Nick and his friends are constantly concocting experiments in the kitchen. A kitchen counter full of molding, foaming broths is not very conducive to food preparation. That's why I advise them to store their potent creations outdoors.

When Mrs. Bown's class gutted a VCR, the kids ended up with a floor covered with wires, motors, circuit boards, and other fascinating gadgetry. Once the class collected these precious treasures, they were put in boxes on a cart in the corner. They became the source of all sorts of real and imaginary inventions.

As you watch kids play, you may realize how exciting tubs of junk can be and not feel so bad about having it around. As you tinker with explorer gear, you too may want it handy. As you explore your home turf, you may also begin to see it as one small corner of a big universe. You may find yourself in a place for exploration.

Searching and Researching

As Nick, Ali, and I climbed over the neighbor's rock wall, Ali shouted, "Mushrooms!" At the base of some live oak trees was a cluster of white-capped mushrooms. Ali picked some and I immediately warned her to keep her fingers away from her mouth. I'm familiar with local mushrooms. Though I knew that these were not deadly, I wanted the kids to be wary of all mushrooms, since I wouldn't always be around to warn them. Ali was picking several mushrooms and said, "I want to get some different kinds." All the mushrooms were the same species, but they had individual differences. Both kids poked and prodded as they selected their mushroom bouquets. As we walked home, fungus in tow, Nick and Ali wanted to know what kinds of mushrooms they had found, but I played dumb. I wanted them to discover that there were other fountains of knowledge besides Mom, Dad, and teacher. At home, I awarded them with a hefty mushroom field guide packed with color photos. Without much prompting, the two four-year-olds started leafing through the pages. I went off to do some chores, and a half hour later they found me and excitedly pointed at a picture of *Armellaria mellea*. From deep within the thousand-page tome, they had correctly identified honey fungus.

Books that relate to interests of the moment are prizes. One class of kindergarten kids who had been playing with worms for several days found a book on the subject. This was an absolute bonanza. The kids attacked their teacher voraciously with questions: "What does this say?" and "Read it to me." CD-ROM, videos, magazines, and computer networks also garner the same responses. Information by itself is dead, but, like a good dry fuel, it feeds the fires of inquiry.

Instruments of Play

Scientists use a variety of tools and instruments to investigate the universe and beyond. When children have a wide array of equipment at hand, they can readily pursue divergent paths. I have often observed children pausing during an investigation to search for the right tool—whether it be tweezers, a stethoscope, or a screwdriver. Below is a list of tools that will help children focus on different avenues of exploration. Though many of these tools may already be in your possession, the key is to make them all easily accessible.

Acrylic tubing—for figuring out flow, gravity, and water pressure

Air pumps—for air play

Blocks—for construction

Compasses—for sensing directions

Cookie cutters and molds—for playing with solids

Cups and containers—for water play

Fans—for moving air

Funnels—for water and air play

Gyroscopes and tops—for revolutionary discoveries

Hair dryer—for exploring air

Hourglasses—for measuring time

Locks and keys—for exploring how locks work

Magnets—for investigating magnetism

Magnifying lenses—for focusing on minutiae (Inexpensive lenses may be best for preschool kids; the better ones are less likely to get scratched by older kids.)

Measuring tapes and rulers—for sizing up things

Musical instruments—for experimenting with sounds

Pendulums—for grappling with gravity

Pinwheels—for air play

Pipe insulation—for making ramps to investigate gravity

Prisms, mirrors, and kaleidoscopes—for light journeys

Pulleys—for further experiences with wheels and friction

PVC pipes—for checking out air and water flow

Record turntable—for spinning things

Scales—for weighing and comparing mass

Screw drivers and pliers—for taking things apart

Stethoscope—for listening

Straws—for air play and construction

Thermometers—for comparing temperatures

Tornado tubes—for observing flow

Toy parachutes—for messing about with flight

Trowels—for archaeology, geology, and wormology

Tweezers—for picking up little things

Water droppers—for focusing on small amounts of liquids

Wind socks, wind vanes, and wind chimes—for observing wind

Making Choices about Choice

Kids are motivated learners. They are curious, inquisitive, natural-born explorers who can easily be stifled by someone else's agenda. As a parent or teacher, it is difficult to deny that kids' interests differ from our own. Despite the fact that each child's interests are unique, schools have operated for many years on the "one size fits all" approach to learning. In science, like other disciplines, all kids were expected to be fascinated by the same materials and methods. On top of this, they were bombarded with facts rather than experience. It wasn't important that kids learn how to learn, only that they learn the information required for each grade level.

During that last decade, there has been a revolution in education, especially at the early childhood level. Those in revolt are parents and teachers who advocate a child-centered education where kids have the opportunity to follow interests. As parents, teachers, and caregivers, we have an important decision to make. Should we place our kids at the wheel or in the back seat? If you are ready to take a true joy ride, keep reading and hand over the key.

One

Playing with water is both relaxing and stimulating. It also keeps you and the kids cool. It's not only fun but can lead to great discoveries about the physical properties of water, hydraulic engineering, gravity, and other things you may have learned in high-school physics. There's so much happening with water play that it needs a permanent place in the lives of young scientists.

Water Droppers

A water dropper is a simple tool that can be the ticket to a whole new theater of water play. Whether investigating water drops and bubbles or experimenting with suction and propulsion, kids will be fascinated.

MATERIALS
Plastic water droppers

Large paper clips with one end straightened

Pebbles, erasers, and other objects such as sticks or leaves

Small plastic containers

The Setup

For indoor use place everything on a table. Fill the containers with water and let the kids go at it. Beware of squirting, however. If you want to allow free reign on squirting and other wet exploits, set up on a table outdoors on a warm day.

Explain to kids why they should not drink the water or poke the droppers in eyes, ears, or nostrils.

The Science

While the kids were playing with the droppers at a picnic table, the father of one of the boys stopped by to see what they were up to. He was at the school checking devices that prevent water contamination. As he watched the kids, he noticed that they were exploring siphons, negative pressure, suction, and other processes that he had to understand to do his job.

What can you do with the droppers? What do you notice about the drops? Why do you think these things happen?

Real Life Science (ages 5–6)

Alex looked at his water dropper and asked, "How do I get water into this thing?"

"Put it in the water and squeeze the top," Nick answered.

Rhyen dripped water onto the stem of a plant and commented, "One fell off, one fell on."

Other kids dripped water onto the pebbles and Rico dripped some onto an eraser. As Jamie dropped water onto a small stone, she said, "I'm going to see if it cleans it off." As Nathan squeezed his bulb in and out, he said, "I like this noise."

When puddles appeared all over the table, Rico drained them with his water dropper. In the process, he discovered he could make bubbles. Nick, who was watching, started making bubbles too.

It wasn't long before one of the kids discovered squirting. Once Matteo shot water across the table, all the kids were trying it. Rico made his shoot highest by placing the bulb of the water dropper between two tables and then pushing them together quickly. Fountains of fine spray arched across the tables.

"Nick, have you done this?" asked Rhyen, displaying a paper clip inserted in the eye dropper. When he quickly depressed the bulb, out moved the clip. Luckily, it only moved to the end of the tube instead of shooting across the room. Soon all the kids were experimenting with water propulsion.

Another day, by chance, both hot and cold water were set out.

"My hot water comes out faster than the cold," said Emmy.

"That's silly," replied Katelyn.

"The cold water makes better noise, but I like the hot water," added Jamie.

"You don't know how to make the song," said Emmy, as she made a rhythm with her dropper. Then other kids began to develop dropper rhythms, and the music of wet discoveries dripped onward.

Water Tubs

Pouring and washing are the basic activities kids will engage in, but providing them with a variety of materials will lead them into deeper explorations. They may invent "water machines," play with bubbles, "paint," make "soup," give baths, and create fountains. Like hydraulic engineers, kids may test different configurations of equipment and develop complex water transfer systems.

MATERIALS

Turkey basters

Sponges and corks

Plastic pitchers and cups

Aluminum pots

Acrylic tubing (see appendix)

Rainmakers (see below)

Plastic bottles, jars, and funnels of different sizes

Dish-washing tubs or water table

Water pumps

Paintbrushes

Plastic animals, cars, and other small toys

Rubber balls

Pebbles and paper clips

The Setup

Make rainmakers by poking holes in the bottom of plastic containers. The water will flow out better if you poke from the inside out. Vary the number and size of holes in different containers. Make funnels by cutting off the tops of narrow-necked plastic bottles. This kit is ideal for use outdoors on a warm day where it can be set up on a lawn, table, or blacktop. If you're indoors, arrange the materials in a space where spilling will not be a problem.

Be sure to let children know that the water they are playing with is not clean enough to drink.

The Science

Your young hydrologists will delve elbow-deep into discoveries with water pressure, evaporation, saturation, and buoyancy. Playing with the acrylic tubes may lead to investigations of how water seeks its own level or how siphons work.

Real Life Science (ages 2–5)

Not many things could be better than messing about with water on a hot day. As kids dipped, dripped, dribbled, and poured, they explored the wonders of water. Two-year-old Ellie busied herself washing some muddy dinosaurs. Kristin poured water from one container to another and Jessica sucked up water with a baster.

Seth discovered an acrylic tube and experimented with it for more than an hour. He drew water up the tube with the baster and created bubbles by blowing into the tube. After inserting a funnel in one end of the tube, Seth placed it against his mouth and cheeks. When he exhaled, air bubbled out the other end. When he inhaled, water siphoned back up the tube. As Seth breathed in and out, he watched his airy work.

Meanwhile, Johnny had discovered that he could use the baster to make water erupt out of a funnel full of water. Isaiah, Seth's older brother, filled a tube with water and blew it out of a funnel attached to the other end. Thrilled with Isaiah's invention, Alex, Sean, and Logan created shoot tubes of their own. As these older boys blasted water, two-year-old Brian blissfully dipped and "painted" with a brush and little Langston stood nearby just watching all the wet workings.

Ice

Investigating ice structure and texture on a hot day is a cool experience. Kids may sculpt and shape the ice, experiment with fracturing it, or become intrigued by ice patterns. They may apply other materials such as water, sand, or grass to the ice and explore the reactions.

MATERIALS
Blocks of ice
Forks and spoons
Spray bottles
Food coloring
Poster paint
Paintbrushes
Large tub or pan
Magnifying lens
Salt (optional)

The Setup

Make ice blocks by freezing water in containers—the bigger the better. Plastic milk jugs or liter bottles with the tops cut off work well. Set the ice-filled containers in the sun or run under hot water to loosen the blocks.

Fill the spray bottles with warm water and add food coloring. Adding salt will make it work faster, but excessive amounts of saltwater used outdoors may damage plants. Warm water by itself will melt ice.

Fill a tub or pan half full of hot water and mix in some poster paint for color. Let kids play with the ice outdoors if possible, otherwise set the ice in a large tub or pan.

The Science

As children observe ice, they may notice its crystalline structure and explore the process of melting. Chipping will lead to discoveries about hardness and fracturing.

Real Life Science (ages 5–7)

"It's hard like metal," Spencer noted as he played with an ice shard. "I made the Atlantic Ocean," Alex told Karena, as he pointed to a pack of miniature icebergs floating in a blacktop puddle.

"It's making little purple dots," Nalani pointed out as she painted her ice chunk. "Look, I made a rainbow."

"It looks like there's grass inside," said Emily as she described the long crystals within her block.

Comments flew with the chips of ice. Great discoveries flowed from the changing ice blocks. Denise, Nalani, and Emily worked together to make holes, while Josh engineered tunnels by himself.

Rico shared ideas on prying the ice apart, and Nick carved his name in the surface with a fork. Alex constructed a puzzle out of chunks of ice and rocks. Later, he joined Rico and Nick in a major ice-melting experiment. Armed with a magnifying lens and tinfoil, the boys tested their ideas about concentrating light. Nick thought the tinfoil would absorb light, so he focused the lens on a foil-covered depression. After uncovering and examining the hole, he announced, "It works!"

Bubbles

ages 2 & up

Bubbles are ethereal jewels, easy both to create and to destroy. Their creation and destruction can be the source of seemingly endless tests. Kids will experiment to discover how big a bubble they can create or how far a bubble will fly. Bubbles will be poked, tickled, and grabbed. Production methods will be examined in detail, reports frequently given, and new ideas will, undoubtedly, bubble forth.

MATERIALS

Dish-washing liquid, such as Dawn or Joy

Plastic six-pack holders

Strawberry baskets

Giant bubble makers (see appendix)

Large tubs or a small plastic swimming pool

Glycerin or Karo syrup (optional)

Food coloring (optional)

The Setup

To make the bubble solution mix 1 cup of dish-washing liquid with 10 cups water. For stronger bubbles, add 3 to 4 tablespoons of glycerin or 2 tablespoons of Karo syrup.

You can add a few drops of food coloring to spice up the potion.

Bubble making is most successful during humid times of the day, such as the morning or evening. Since trees give off humidity, setting up in the shade of a large tree during midday is another choice.

The Science

Bubbleology can lead to great investigations of air and light. Examining what causes bubbles to pop may lead to observations about heat, wind, or surface tension. For example, since warm, dry air absorbs water, bubbles pop as they come in contact with it. As children blow bubbles, they will have a chance to observe the effects of air pressure or to observe the honeycomb-like patterns of connected bubbles. Peering at the surface of bubbles can lead to examination of the color spectrum and experiments with reflections.

Real Life Science (ages 2–5)

Isaiah looked at Logan and stated with conviction that bubbles could not be made by blowing. They must, he stated, be swung into creation. Moments later, Logan blew some bubbles and continued to blow, without saying anything to Isaiah.

Meanwhile, Sef tried to empty out a jug full of bubbles. While a little liquid poured out, the bulk of the froth just clung to the interior. Shake as Sef might, the bubbles held tightly to the container. Alex also experimented with the clinging properties of bubbles as he shook them off his fingers. Small bubbles departed with each forceful shake. Johnny dipped his fingers in a bubbly cup and also flicked them off. Nearby, Brogan filled a cup with suds and continually poured them over one of his hands. Ellie dropped sand on her bubbles.

Alex watched intently as he prodded bubbles with his fingertips. The rainbow-hued skin stretched in and out. Amazingly, few broke. Alex nudged his nose against a giant bubble. "I felt the bubble," he announced.

Isaiah blew bubbles and then tried to catch them. Using a ring and pan, he then discovered how to draw out large bubbles. As he watched the bubble grow, he exclaimed to some nearby kids, "I'm making tornadoes." Several children came over to see how the skin of the bubbles narrowed to a cone before transforming into a sphere.

Boats

When you invite kids to design a boat with a wide array of materials, they will respond with enthusiasm and act with ingenuity. Get ready to watch some very creative applications of understandings of buoyancy.

MATERIALS
Tinfoil

Paper plates

Cups, Styrofoam, and other discarded packing materials

Straws and clay

Pieces of foam

Pieces of sponge

Corks

The Setup

Provide the materials and let kids go for it. If you don't have corks at home, you can ask a restaurant if they have any that you can have. If puddles are not available, set out a wading pool. If possible, leave the boats out for a while.

The Science

Kids will share ideas, invent, and test. This is real experimentation. Properties of materials will be tested and compared. Kids will learn about such things as porousness, density, impermeability, and general seaworthiness. No kidding.

Real Life Science (ages 5–8)

It had been raining for days. Monster puddles inhabited the soaked playground. It was time for boats. It didn't take long for materials to become scattered across the floor as kids built as intensely as bees. Boats came together as ideas were exchanged and techniques mastered. The best method of inserting mast straws through paper or foam hulls made its way around the entire group. The designs constantly metamorphosed as children watched each other, but each boat was a unique creation. Each boat would either sink or float. Hypotheses were abundant.

"Your boat isn't gonna work."

"It might not sink you know."

When boats were ready for the first voyage, kids enthusiastically took them to the playground waters. Though it was raining gently, the kids didn't notice the drops as they launched the fleet of strange and wonderful ships. In the puddle sea, the boats bobbed, drifted, lilted, and tilted. Some sank. Rico said he wanted to make a boat that sank. When launched, it did indeed rest on the bottom.

"See," Rico commented, "It's too heavy." Then he went inside to make another boat.

No one had ever designed anything like these unique vessels. Elizabeth's unsinkable cruiser consisted of a plate with a ring of corks taped on top. Ali's resembled a buoy with a TV antennae.

The next day, the puddle looked like the resting grounds of the Spanish Armada. It was littered with boat parts, sinking vessels, and totally submerged wrecks. Kids shared ideas about why certain boats sank.

"It got soaked."

"It fell apart."

"Waves smashed it."

We cleared up the wreckage and stored ideas for new designs for another rainy day.

Plumbing

ages 3 & up

Kids are natural-born plumbers. Whether it's water swirling down a drain or an outgoing tide, kids love to play with flowing water. PVC pipes, acrylic tubing, funnels, and fittings are the perfect answer to their plumbing dreams. Considering the time most kids will devote to messing about with the plumbing, you'll feel fortunate you don't have to pay for their labor. The other good news is that these materials are relatively inexpensive, indestructible, and available at the local hardware store.

MATERIALS

10 or more feet of ½-inch PVC pipe

10 or more 90-degree fittings for ½-inch pipes

10 or more 120-degree fittings for ½-inch pipe

10 or more T-fittings for ½-inch pipes

Three 2- to 4-foot lengths of clear acrylic tubing (choose sizes that funnels will fit into)

10 funnels of various sizes

Several small, plastic tubs and cups

Small pieces of old kitchen sponges

Several buckets or large tubs

Corks

The Setup

Cut the pipe in a variety of short lengths (8, 10, 12, and 18 inches). Most hardware stores have special cutters for PVC pipe, but you can also use a hacksaw. Funnels can be made by cutting off the tops of narrow-necked plastic bottles. Corks are available from restaurants; just ask a local eatery to save them for you!

This is a perfect activity for the warmer seasons. If possible, place the materials outside where spilling water won't be a problem. Easy access to an outdoor water spigot will also come in handy.

Before allowing kids to use the pipes, elicit ideas on how to use them safely. Let kids know that they should not use the pipes for hitting or whacking. Fill the buckets and tubs with water, and let kids go at it.

The Science

Children will investigate the physical properties of water, such as water pressure and fluid mechanics. This is a great opportunity for group problem solving and inventing.

Real Life Science (ages 5–6)

Within the first few minutes, the children were building everything from megaphones to water filters to "pumps." Nathan placed a funnel on top of a short section of the pipe and called out, "Attention, attention." This looked like fun to Spencer and Emily, and soon all three were walking around spouting "Attention!"

Meanwhile, Rhyen attempted to move water from one container to another with a section of acrylic tubing. "Nothing came through," he announced to no one in particular. Later, he raised the hose in the middle to get the water to move, but still none came through. "That's funny," he muttered.

Emmy came by and began to dip a cup into one of the tubs that Rhyen was using. "That's mine," Rhyen asserted, but Emmy continued to dip water despite his protest. "Attention, attention," Nathan, Spencer, and Emily continued announcing through their megaphones. Nick had found a funnel to fit inside his tube and was pouring cup after cup down it. "It's coming out the other end," observed Spencer. Nick just kept pouring and didn't reply.

Josh sat on the ground and pieced tube after tube together until his creation dwarfed his own small figure. "That bucket is mine," Rhyen persisted as Emmy continued to transfer water from one container to another.

Matteo came out, looked around, and asked, "What can I do to help?" He surveyed several projects and ended up assisting Nick. As a whole crew of other kids came out, the dynamics of the play changed. Rico joined Rhyen, who, now having a part-ner, began concentrating more on creating with Rico than on chasing off Emmy. Katie, Katelyn, and Ali immediately began building a contraption with a funnel on top. Katie reported, "We were expecting the water to come out here, but it came out there." The three girls busily retrofitted their device until the water went where they wanted it to go. As Katie was struggling to put two pieces together without a fitting to join them, Rhyen handed her a coupling and asked, "Is this what you need?"

Nick and Matteo's device had changed into a "water filter," and Alex provided them with many ideas: "Why don't we put a sponge here?" "What if we filter gray water?" Soon the boys were collecting spilled water from the asphalt and "recycling" it for further use.

On other days, kids made complex water delivery systems, played with shooting water out of the tubing, and even made contraptions to water the bushes.

Tornado Tubes

ages 3 & up

Becoming familiar with how the tubes work will lead to problem-solving symposiums and endless trial-and-error experiments. Observations may stimulate animated discussions of past experiences with draining bathtubs and sinks, as well as theories about tornadoes and other swirling motions.

MATERIALS

Tornado tubes (see appendix)

Liter or quart plastic soda bottles

Glitter (optional)

Food coloring (optional)

The Setup

Fill one bottle two-thirds full of water and screw the tornado tube onto this bottle. (You can also add a pinch or two of glitter and a drop of food coloring.) Attach an empty bottle to the other end of the tube.

Set the empty bottle upright on a flat surface so that the full bottle is on top. Demonstrate how to set the tornado in motion by shaking the top bottle briefly in a circular motion.

The Science

A vortex is a swirling flow of water or other liquid. When water drops through a hole, its moving energy is concentrated into a smaller area causing a spiral flow. As the water molecules come closer to the opening, the rotation becomes greater and generates an outward force. The resulting centrifugal force keeps the water out of the exact center of the opening. Playing with the tornado tubes provides children with more opportunities to explore the effects of gravity on the movement of liquids.

Real Life Science (ages 5–7)

"I just shake it like this," Karena explained to her friends.

David displayed his swirling waters to Josh, "It's fixed now." Josh complained, "It's not coming at all," and he stopped playing with it. Rico wondered, "How is it supposed to go down? Oh, it has a little hole. Oooh, there's a tornado."

Eyeing several aqueous tornadoes, Zachary commented that they varied in size.

After shaking his tube for five minutes, David exclaimed, "Ah, it's coming out."

Rico and David compared the speed of the flow and very soon they were racing tornadoes. Young spectators gathered around to discover the winner.

"Come on twister!" David rooted for his tornado.

Kid Science Library

Fiction

Allen, Pamela. *Who Sank the Boat?* New York: Coward, 1985.

A boat sinks when five animal friends go on an outing.

Carlstrom, Nancy White. *Better Not Get Wet, Jesse Bear.* New York: MacMillan, 1988.

A nice book to accompany water play and to set the stage for discussing when and what to get wet.

Cooney, Barbara. *Hattie and the Waves.* New York: Scholastic, 1992.

A wavy romp. Let children make an ocean with a paint roller pan (or plastic wading pool), sand, and water where they can play at making waves.

Dabovich, Lydia. *Busy Beavers.* New York: Scholastic, 1989.

This tale of dam builders encourages kids to follow suit. Allow kids to collect materials to make small dams in the garden on hose-made streams.

Dabovich, Lydia. *Follow the River.* New York: Dutton, 1980.

A river travelogue from beginning to the sea. Provide kids with tools and water so they can construct a river in the sand or soil.

Dalton, Shelia. *Bubblemania.* Point Roberts, WA: Orca, 1992.

A little boy creates an enormous bubble that takes off and swallows all kinds of things, including the baby next door!

Martin, Bill. *Listen to the Rain.* New York: Holt, 1988.

A meditation on the changing sounds of rain. Read during a rainstorm to stimulate observation.

Mayer, Mercer. *Bubble, Bubble.* Roxbury, CT: Rainbird, 1973.

After a boy buys a bubble maker, he discovers it can blow bubbles in the shape of everything from floating kangaroos to charging elephants.

Poskanzer, Susan Cornell. *The Great Bubble Ride.* Mahwah, NJ: Troll Associates, 1986.

An imaginary tale to go with real bubble adventures.

Ross, Michael Elsohn. *Cycles, Cycles, Cycles*. El Portal, CA: Yosemite Association, 1979.

The "Water Cycle" chapter serves as a good follow-up to water dropper play and observations of condensation.

Shulevitz, Uri. *Rain, Rain Rivers*. New York: Farrar, Straus and Giroux, 1969.

A young girl narrates the trip rain takes, beginning by falling on her house and ending at the sea.

Thaler, Mike. *In the Middle of a Puddle*. New York: Harper Trophy, 1988.

This puddle story will tell kids it's OK to make and play with puddles.

Wild, Margaret. *There's a Sea in My Bedroom*. Worthington, OH: Willowisp, 1987.

David, who is afraid of the sea, finds a conch shell and can hear the sea inside it. He imagines the sea leaving the shell and entering his bedroom.

Nonfiction

Pollock, Penny. *Water Is Wet*. New York: Putnam's, 1985.

A basic survey of water and its properties.

Earth & Other Matter

From the very beginning, kids mess about with matter. As babies, they mash, knead, sniff, and smear whatever they can get their hands on. Kids like to explore "stuff." The more they play with materials such as mud or wet sand, the more they learn about what they do and what can be done with them. Gloop, oobleck, and other unusual substances challenge children to explore and compare. These materials act differently from anything they have played with before. Perhaps they are like snot but not really snotty. Maybe they feel like rubber, but rubber doesn't break as easily. With little or no encouragement, children will begin to compare the different stuff and develop theories to explain its behavior. This may lead children to a higher level of questions best tackled by university physics or chemistry instructors. Don't worry if you don't have answers. Just roll up your sleeves, dig in, and join in some goopy, gloopy pondering.

Rocks

Rocks are rich in texture, mass, and color. Children may discover that they can scratch rocks with the paper clips or scribble on tiles with rocks. Rocks may end up being dipped and "weighed" or peered at through lenses. Kids may use them in imaginative play or simply touch them with inquisitive little fingers.

MATERIALS
Balance scales

Large paper clips

Unglazed tile (scraps available from tile shops)

Variety of rocks

Large tub of water

Watercolor brushes

Magnifying lenses

The Setup

Collect or purchase a variety of rocks, such as quartz, slate, pumice, sandstone, limestone, and marble. Straighten one end of each paper clip. Fill the tub one or two inches deep with water.

Before the kids begin playing, discuss with them how to use the magnifying lenses and how to protect them from becoming scratched.

The Science

As children play with a variety of rocks, they will begin to compare them. These comparisons may lead to discoveries in hardness, texture, density, and color. Control your impulse to ask leading questions. Ask reflective questions instead, especially when kids share discoveries. For example, if a child shows you how water changes the color of a rock, you might ask, "Have you noticed that before?"

Real Life Science (ages 2–5)

Hannah carefully "painted" some rocks with water and revealed striking patterns and color. Sean peered at one through a lens. Ellie busily transferred rocks from tubs to scales and back. Tiles were painted, slid, and spun on the wet tabletop. Rocks were swished in the water. Kristin dropped some rocks in the water, and Joshie, who was standing on the sidelines hugging two stuffed animals, commented to his teacher Cindy, "She put the rocks in the water."

Cindy replied, "In the water, rocks get wet."

"They sink," Joshie added.

Johnny put a tile on a brush handle and tried to balance it.

"Look, this is a truck thing; it flies in the air. It broked off." Johhny then proceeded to use the brush in imaginative play. Within a period of fifteen minutes, it transformed from a shark to a whale to a rocket and finally to a bell.

Joshie, still clutching his horse and bear at the periphery, asked, "What if you stuck the brush all the way in?"

Johnny left and Ellie had the tub to herself. In went rocks and out dripped water.

"There's not enough water in there," observed Joshie.

When the table was vacant, Joshie stepped up to the table for a closer look, but he did not touch anything. A couple of weeks later, Joshie came to the table with his hands free and joined in with a group of other children.

As the crowd thinned out, five-year-old Eddie grabbed all the rocks, tiles, and paper clips, and dropped them in. Swishing back and forth like he was panning for gold, he created a noticeable racket. Johnny took a couple of magnifying lenses and started to drum on the balance scale buckets. Hannah got the other buckets and some lenses to join in. It was rock music at its finest.

Sand Play

Sand alone will keep most kids occupied. Adding a variety of tools brings more depth and complexity to their play. Gutters, ramps, and pulleys may lead to group construction projects, while sifters and magnets stimulate sorting. Rainmakers and buckets allow kids to experiment with erosion, percolation, and flowing water.

MATERIALS

Large magnets

Food containers of various sizes

Cookie cutters and molds

Plastic gutter and down spout

Quart yogurt containers

Bucket of water

Pipe insulation ramps (see appendix)

Pulleys (see appendix)

Trowels or small sand shovels

The Setup

You can create rainmakers by poking holes in the bottoms and lower sides of the plastic containers with an ice pick or nail. Attach yarn or string to magnets to help keep track of them in the sand.

The Science

Sand play is an investigation of the physical properties of sand. Pouring sand down a gutter or ramp provides a chance to explore friction. Sifting sand and playing with magnets reveals characteristics of sandy components. Adding water to sand play adds new experiences with erosion, saturation, and adhesion. Considering the global problems with topsoil loss and groundwater contamination it seems adults could also benefit from more time in the sandbox wrestling with these topics.

Mud Play

ages 2 & up

Kids and pigs adore mud. Mud lends itself to endless investigation and dramatic play. Not only will kids concoct mud pies and dirt cakes, but they will experiment with consistency. Is it brushable, pourable, or sliceable?

MATERIALS
Food containers of various sizes
Cookie cutters and molds
Pie plates, muffin tins, and pans
Spoons, spatulas, and butter knives
Plastic food containers
Bucket of water
Trowels or small sand shovels
Paintbrushes and sponge brushes
Gutters

The Setup

This is definitely an outside activity best set up where a muddy mess is perfectly acceptable. Any patch of bare ground with accessible water will do.

Kids decorated with mud may look monstrously dirty, when in fact they are easy to wash off. During hot weather, you can simply hose down mucky kids into cleanliness. At cleanup time, set out a bucket of clean water for rinsing hands.

The Science

Messing about in the mud can lead to major discoveries in the fields of physics, soil science, and imaginary baking. Mud play can lead children to discoveries about texture, flow, permeability, absorption, and evaporation.

Real Life Science (ages 2–6)

Mud beckons. Despite the fact that the kids had been mucking about in the yard for months, each succeeding day brought new adventures.

As Sean excavated a mud pit, Alex worked in some saturated sand with a hoe and announced, "I'm making concrete."

Nearby, Timmy poured water down an inclined 10-foot length of gutter. Josh came bouncing over and said, "Remember what we did Thursday?"

Soon Josh was piecing together a downspout and gutter and "cementing" them with mud. "Have to lock them real good, 'cause the water makes holes," Josh explained.

After peering at Sean's pit, Alex asked, "How deep is that?"

Sean didn't answer as he poured water in the pit.

"It's gonna overflow," Alex predicted, but it didn't. No matter how many buckets Sean poured, the water just disappeared. Alex suggested channeling water from the gutter into the pit and soon he'd made an aqueduct. Josh continued tinkering with "locking" the gutter and downspout together with mud. As he poured water down the gutter, the mud kept washing away.

Jason came over with a brush and began painting the gutter with mud and Josh soon abandoned his work to assist in coating the gutter.

Ellie, Kristin, Kelly, Billy, and Jessica sat in a circle like a quilting bee "baking" mud cakes and pies. Kelly called her oozy pie, a "hot" pie. Alex brought over "frosting" for the cakes. Sef not only took an offered slice of pie, but tasted it as well. Unfortunately, it didn't taste as good as it looked and was immediately ejected.

Gloop

Not only is gloop inexpensive and easy to make, but it will intrigue both adults and kids for days. From the moment kids encounter gloop, they try to figure out if it is **Silly Putty**, gack, or some other known substance. As they stretch, tug, mash, roll, and break it, kids discover the unique qualities of this new substance.

MATERIALS
Borax

White glue

Watercolor or poster paint (optional)

Large bowl

3 cups

Measuring cup

Wooden spoon

Small toys and other objects, such as shells, pattern blocks, and cookie cutters

The Setup

Mix up some gloop:

1. Add 1½ cups of water to 2 cups glue.

2. Pour ⅓ cup of warm water into 3 cups. (Optional: Add a drop or two of watercolor or poster paint for color.)

3. Stir a teaspoon of borax into each cup.

4. One at a time, pour the contents of each cup into the glue and water mixture. Mix until it's dissolved.

Despite the fact that this stuff is made with glue, it is not sticky. In fact, it is quite unmessy. Provide a clean table for kids to sit at. This will keep the gloop clean. Of course, if you choose to produce a large supply, let kids use it outside to see how it reacts with natural materials. Store gloop in an airtight container to prevent it from drying out. Make sure that the kids clean it up carefully because, if not detected, it will melt, harden, and become difficult to remove.

The Setup

Kids will delve into the "icities," such as plasticity and elasticity. They may also ponder tensile strengths, malleability, and oozeability.

Real Life Science (ages 5–7)

As soon as the children had it in their hands, they were busy discussing its unusual properties.

"It's like a bouncing ball."

"It breaks."

"You can make string!"

"It feels like it's wet, but it isn't."

"It makes bubbles."

"It melts."

"Don't chew it or you'll throw up."

Rico commented, "It glues together."

"It's glue," Matteo replied.

"It's made with glue," Katie said.

"It's snot," one of the girls said while giggling and holding a stringy piece near her nostrils.

There were also lots of names for it, from gunk to goop to gack. It was pounded, stretched, rolled, bounced, and cut. Rico stretched some into string and pretended it was a snake. He made the snake hiss at Humberto, and Humberto laughed.

Toy dinosaurs and other small objects that had been set near the kids were soon incorporated into the investigations. Ali used pattern blocks to make impressions, Nathan made dinosaur footprints, and Rico pressed in a key.

"Humberto, it's eating it," Rico shouted, but Humberto didn't notice. He was busy feeding gloop to his toy dinosaur.

As kids discovered properties of gloop, they spread the information around the table. For example, the discovery that gloop could produce the sounds of flatulence was instantly communicated to all.

Nick held a big piece in front of his mouth, and with a greedy look on his face he said to Emmy, "What if this was all gum? Yummy."

Oobleck

ages 2 & up

At first, kids may shy away from oobleck. It looks, feels, and acts strange. It's gooey and messy. Oobleck is repulsive, yet attractive. Within minutes, kids may move from tentative touches to handling it in handfuls because, like many messy things, it's incredibly fun to play with.

Luckily for adults, oobleck is also easy to make and clean up. When you play with it outside, all you need is a hose to wash the drips and dribbles away. Oobleck gets its name from *Bartholomew and the Oobleck*, a Dr. Seuss story about a strange substance concocted by wizards. With this great literature tie-in, you can easily extend the dramatic play and lead children into discussions of noxious and toxic substances.

MATERIALS
Cornstarch, at least two boxes
Dish-washing tub
Wooden spoon
Spatula or trowels for scraping up dried oobleck
Bucket
Poster paint or food coloring

The Setup

Mix small amounts of cornstarch and water until you get a mixture that is both dry and liquid at once. Add a small amount of paint or food coloring. The color will be pale because of the cornstarch.

Oobleck is best played with outdoors or on a table that is easy to wash. As it is spilled onto tables, it will began to dry out. If kids don't realize they can put it back into the tubs, you can show them how to recycle it.

Outdoor messes can be hosed away. Use a bucket of warm water to rinse off the kids' hands when they are finished playing.

The Science

Playing with oobleck encourages kids to explore the differences between liquids and solids since oobleck, unlike other substances, seems to be both at once.

Real Life Science (ages 2–12)

"Sick! Gross! Ooooh!" kids commented, but they couldn't keep their fingers out of the stuff.

Nalani dripped it. Lea watched, mesmerized, as she swirled her fingers through it. Jamie rubbed it all over her hands.

"It looks like water, but it isn't," exclaimed two-and-a-half-year-old Nissa.

"It's hard, but it drips," said her four-year-old sister Dana.

"When you pick it up, it goes to bits," commented twelve-year-old Jacob.

"Wow, it's hard," said five-year-old Claire.

This strange stuff doesn't behave as expected and leads to endless experimentation. Rico tried to make a ball and then announced, "The ball is melting!" Rhyen said, "If I touch it, it will melt."

"It's hard to make a ball. You need to move it all the time or it will go all over the place."

For 15 minutes, Rhyen made oobleck pancakes and then watched them melt. Then he dropped bits of oobleck into water and watched it.

Oobleck is also great for creative play. Nalani pretended she was making witches' brew. Ali, Katie, and Katelyn constructed a candy machine by pouring oobleck through each other's hands, while Nick pretended he had vanilla frosting on his fingers.

Magnets

Though magnets are familiar to most kids, few have had the opportunity for extensive play with a wide variety of magnets and materials. The more kids are able to play with different kinds of magnets and materials, the more their minds will magnetically attract new questions and theories. This kit is a virtual smorgasbord of magnets. Luckily, compared with most other science equipment, magnets are both reasonably priced and durable.

MATERIALS
Various kinds of magnets

Nuts, bolts, and other little pieces of metal and nonmetal objects

Box of paper clips

Pieces of cardboard or index cards

Box lids

The Setup

One source of free magnets is a broken VCR or another piece of electronic equipment. If your kids have already done "Disassembly Line" (p.91), scavenge the parts for magnets and other objects. Special magnets, such as magnetic marbles and floating magnets, are available from companies listed in the "Resources" appendix.

Set up everything at a table or on the floor.

The Science

As kids play with magnets, they will discover that magnets have poles, that they vary in strength, and that they are attracted to a certain class of materials. Kids will develop their own explanations for these different aspects of magnetic attractions without knowing the scientific terms. Though it's not important to teach any terms, you can facilitate their wonderings with some of your own and join in on the play. Questions like "I wonder why that happened" or "I wonder what would happen if I did this" may help stimulate more thinking.

Real Life Science (ages 5–8)

"Look, look, look," was all the kids said to each other for the first few minutes. Each had something to show about their magnet. Alex used a magnet mounted on a long handle to extract paper clips from a box. Rhyen used his horseshoe magnet to drag marbles around the table. Rico tested to see how many things his magnet could hold. Ali put her wand-like magnet under the table and moved paper clips on the top surface. Then she tried the same thing with her hand. "It goes through my hand," she announced. Nalani watched her and tried the same thing with her hand. "It works better on my hand when I use two clips," Nalani exclaimed. Soon, others were trying the hand trick.

The play was constantly changing and varied. Melissa made a little snowman-type toy with two magnetic marbles with a screw for a head. Allison and Jennifer used paper clips on a large index card as puppets and moved them with magnets placed under the card. Ali moved the magnet over a pile of paper clips trying to move them without touching them.

The magnets readily inspired testing and experiments. As soon as Ricky arrived at the table, he started picking up screws with his magnet. One of them wouldn't stick, so he picked it up and put it on the magnet. It fell off. He put it on again, and again it fell off. After the third try, he left it there and moved on to some other screws. Melissa started off by testing to see if the magnets would stick to her head. Elizabeth tested to see how many magnetic marbles she could hang in a chain and Melissa repeated the test.

Rico was busy playing with two magnets. "It's not pulling," he said to Alex, "it's pushing." He kept trying to make them go together and finally shouted, "I got it in the middle. I pushed it."

Kid Science Library

Fiction

Baylor, Byrd. *Everyone Needs a Rock*. New York: Scribner's, 1974.

A guide to finding a rock for a friend. Do what the book suggests!

Baylor, Byrd. *If You Are a Hunter of Fossils*. New York: Scribner's, 1984.

A child imagines the ancient past. Use this book to jump off into a study of paleontology. Obtain some fossils for students to observe. Bury some chicken bones and set up a dig for students to discover "fossilized bones."

Branley, Franklyn, and Eleanor Vaughn. *Mickey's Magnet*. New York: Scholastic, 1956.

Read as a way to stimulate discussion after children have had the opportunity to explore a variety of magnets.

Buchanan, Elizabeth. *Mole Moves House*. New York: Doubleday, 1989.

An exuberant mole refuses to believe his human neighbors think he is a pest. A great lead into explorations of subterranean critters.

Cohen, Carol. *The Mud Pony*. New York: Scholastic, 1988.

These Pawnee origin stories could get your kids making their own mud ponies.

dePaola, Tomie. *The Quicksand Book*. New York: Holiday, 1977.

Discusses the composition of quicksand, rescue procedures, and how to make your own.

Lionni, Leo. *Alexander and the Wind Up Mouse*. New York: Random House, 1969.

A mouse changes a toy mouse into a real mouse when he gives a lizard a purple pebble. After reading this book, challenge children to find unusual colored pebbles.

Lobel, Arnold. *Small Pig.* New York: Harper and Row, 1969.

A pig who has had his pig pen cleaned up by the farmer's wife goes off in search of mud and discovers that good mud is hard to find. A book to go with mud pie making.

Peters, Lisa. *The Sun, the Wind and the Rain.* New York: Holt, 1988.

A side-by-side narration of how the earth makes a mountain (shaping it with the sun, wind, and rain) and a child's efforts at the beach to make a tall sand mountain (which is also affected by the elements). Read after children have done some sand play.

Seuss, Dr. *Bartholomew and the Oobleck.* New York: Random House, 1949.

A cautionary tale about wishing for strange substances. Read this after kids have played with gloop and oobleck.

Steig, William. *Sylvester and the Magic Pebble.* New York: Simon and Schuster, 1969.

Sylvester turns himself into a rock by mistake. A great springboard into pretending to be rocks.

Nonfiction

Rhodes, Frank T. *Geology.* New York: Golden Press, 1972.

A compact, fact-filled guide to geology.

Shaffer, Paul R. And Herbert S. Zim. *Rocks and Minerals.* New York: Golden Press, 1957.

Williams, Claudette, and David Evans. *Magnets and Batteries.* New York: Dorling Kindserley, 1993.

One of the Let's Explore Science series. Plenty of pictures and questions.

Wood, Tim. *Natural Disasters.* New York: Thompson Learning, 1993.

Covers wind, volcanoes, mud slides, avalanches, and meteorites. Let kids make a play town by a mountainside and investigate the properties and effects of a mini-mud slide.

Air

Three

Air is familiar yet mysterious. It can't be snatched with fingers, but it can be pushed and shoved. Though walking on it is difficult, floating or gliding through it is possible with the right equipment. Free, it won't support us, yet if it's captured in a tire or air mattress, it's as reliable as stone. Children occasionally encounter toys and tools that enable them to explore the air. Imagine how daily studies with this equipment could produce some genuine "air head" explorers.

Air Time

Equipped with a menagerie of airy tools, kids will explore the invisible air. With vacuums, they'll suck it in, and with air pumps they'll compress it. With hair dryers, tubes, and straws, they'll blow it out. With fans, they'll push it, and, with pinwheels, they'll put it to work. With plungers, they'll struggle against the immense weight of our atmosphere. They may even combine a variety of tools as they drift further into the realm of airy discovery.

MATERIALS
Bicycle pump
Straws and acrylic tubing
Small plungers
Hair dryer (optional)
Cordless vacuum
Funnels
Ping-Pong balls
Hand-held fans
Pinwheels

The Setup

To make your own fans and pinwheels, see the appendix. If you plan to use the hair dryer, set the materials up near an electrical outlet. You can purchase an old hair dryer at a garage sale and, on some models, it's possible to disconnect the heat element. For health reasons, discourage children from sharing straws.

Unfortunately, vacuums, plungers, and other household air tools are seldom accessible toys for children. When given the opportunity to playfully explore with these tools, children may find themselves seriously investigating air. Whether they delve into force, compression, or vacuums (the concept, as well as the tool), kids will gain more experience with the gas we live with.

What did you discover? Could you show me? Will it happen again? Why?

Real Life Science (ages 5–7)

"It hums," declared Claire as she puffed on her pinwheel. Huffing and puffing as furiously as the Big Bad Wolf, Claire tested the speed limits of her pinwheel.

"It goes fast," she breathlessly exclaimed.

Isaiah's pinwheel zoomed too as he blew through a straw. When Spencer directed the hot breath of a hair dryer on Denise's pinwheel, it whirred with a sustained speed.

David was huffing and puffing too, but not from breeze making. With enough effort to lift the table, David attempted to remove a plunger from the tabletop. Despite his full-on exertion, the plunger held as fast as a lamprey or leech. Inspired by a little success at moving the plunger sideways, David shifted all his power to a side push and off he flew with the released plunger. Again and again he experimented with this contradiction in gripping abilities. Isaiah, who was playing with the other plunger, told David as he plunged the air, "I'm plugging my stove."

Meanwhile, Josh lifted the pump plunger and watched as it slowly drifted downward. He repeated it again and then helped it along. "It goes slow," he said.

Windy Day Party

Discovering the power of the wind is one of the serious pursuits of childhood. Using their own energy as well as the wind, kids will investigate the air. They may tune into the wind's intensity, direction, or even the scents that it carries.

MATERIALS
Pinwheels

Wind wands (see appendix)

Flags

Kites

Toy sailboats

The Setup

If you don't want to purchase pinwheels, you can make some quite easily (see appendix). To make wind wands, see appendix.

Wind socks, weather vanes, simple anemometers, and wind chimes can all be given permanent locations at home or school. These tools will alert kids to the intensity of air movements and may set air explorations into motion.

The Science

Everything from the relative wind speed to wind direction will be the subject of young kids' scrutiny. As kids play with wind toys, they will discover and apply concepts about the nature of the wind. Who knows, perhaps these discoveries will lead to careers as sailors, kite flyers, or even weather forecasters.

Real Life Science (ages 3–7)

The breezy fall afternoon at the play park was a perfect time for the "windy day party." Matteo set the wind wands upright in a gopher mound and watched the dancing ribbons. Nick raced up and down the field catching air in a plastic bag attached to a dried sunflower stalk. Three-year-old Nikita held three pinwheels firmly in her hand. Occasionally she shook and blew on them. Claire held a larger one and blew into it. It moved slowly until she turned it into the wind. As it whirled, Claire exclaimed, "The wind blowed it for me, it did!"

Later, she ran to her house and returned with paper and pens. With a delighted grin, she explained, "I know a wind thing. We can make airplanes."

Airplane construction began immediately as Claire and Nick fashioned simple models from the paper. Once launched, they flew more due to the breeze than engineering.

With the flare of circus performers, Brook and Matteo dashed about waving fluttering wind wands. Like rippling flags, the ribbons gave voice to the wind. Leaves fluttered. Paper blew across the grass. Kids whirled and swirled with the frisky breeze.

Balloons

Balloons festively invite kids to explore air. Kids can bat and bounce them into flight. They can be puffed up, unpuffed, and repuffed. They can make strange sounds and move in odd ways. Kids' play may resemble a party as they celebrate these intriguing bags of air.

MATERIALS
Punchball balloons
Party balloons
Yarn or string

The Setup

Blow up balloons to different degrees of fullness. Hang several pairs of balloons different places. If they are at equal heights and low enough for kids to touch, children will be able to observe the effects of static electricity.

Be sure to alert children to the dangers of placing balloons in their mouths or popping them near their faces.

The Science

The blowing up and deflating balloon leads to discoveries in air pressure. As balloons deflate, kids may explore jet propulsion or airy music. They may invent fans or blowers. Balloon play may also guide kids in exploring the "magical" properties of static electricity or aerodynamics.

Real Life Science (ages 5–7)

Two balloons hung from the ceiling and rested far apart from each other. Without commenting on this odd phenomenon, Timmy and Miguel began tapping the balloons. After they left, Humberto walked by and noticed that one of the balloons moved toward him.

He pushed it away gently and stood mesmerized as it returned to his side. He stepped back and it followed. Again he patted it away, and again it returned. As Josh walked by, Humberto called to him, described the balloon's behavior, and then repeated the test.

Emmy walked about while blowing up her balloon and listened to the air fizzle out. As she stretched the opening, the noise changed in pitch and volume. Emily chased her errant balloons around the room after blowing them up and letting them go. Claire used a straw to blow up her balloon.

The balloons also became incorporated into imaginative play. "See my parachute," Spencer announced, as he jumped off a step with a balloon on a string trailing behind. Moments later, he called out, "Look at my doggy" while he led his balloon on a fast spin about the room.

Flying

Children awarded with a variety of flying equipment may surprise you with an air show of complex and even comical proportions. Parachutes may drag behind runners or be held high above the head by jumpers. At one time or another, most things will be tossed in the air. A large lawn is ideal for this kind of enthusiastic experimentation.

MATERIALS

Parachutes (see appendix)

Whirlybirds (see appendix)

Maple samaras and other flying seeds or pods

Paper clips

Metal washers of various sizes

Feathers

The Setup

Collect the flying seeds from local plants such as dandelions, milkweeds, maples, ashes, acacias, or redbuds. Assemble the parachutes and paper helicopters (see appendix). Demonstrate how items can be attached to the parachutes with the paper clips.

The Science

Surface to volume ratios, air resistance, and the design for flight apparatus are some of the aspects of aerodynamics that children may investigate as they are playing with flying stuff.

Real Life Science (ages 5–8)

It was a beautiful spring day, a perfect day for flight. Carrol attached several washers to his parachute and tossed it into the air. When it plunged downward, he exclaimed, "It has too much weight." Meanwhile, Elizabeth spun around in circles watching her parachute fill with air. Soon she and Melissa were running about with the parachutes trailing behind them. Other kids joined in and there was soon a dashing crew of air draggers.

Alex placed a parachute on his head and said, "I'm going to try it on myself." He jumped off some low bleachers but didn't float. "That gives me an idea," Carrol replied. "I can jump off and then let go." Carrol climbed up on the bleachers and let go of his chute while he leapt. The parachute floated to the lawn. Maira jumped off too, but held onto her chute. Other children climbed up on the bleachers and tossed off seed pods, paper whirlybirds, and parachutes. Nick attached a whirlybird to a parachute and noticed that the parachute lines got twisted.

Later, Carrol discovered that if he added more weight to the parachute, wrapped it into a ball, and then tossed it high in the air that it would float bet-

ter. Kids kept adding weights until they added so many that the parachutes just plummeted to the lawn. Up and down the chutes went.

Some of the kids began putting two chutes together to see if they would work. Many of them became tangled.

Ricky and Rico became excited about flying a foam football. They wondered if they could make it fly. After attaching two parachutes, they tossed it high. Up it went and down it crashed. When they added another chute, the football drifted slowly down like an Apollo space capsule returning to earth.

Sound Play

ages 3 & up

Exploration is not always a quiet pursuit, especially when it comes to exploring sound. As children blow, pound, and pluck a variety of sound-making equipment, they will soon begin to sort and classify the sounds. They will investigate how sound is made.

All the materials that you need to purchase for this exploration kit may be used in other kits. You can easily find or make the rest at home.

MATERIALS

PVC pipe and fittings
(see Plumbing, p.33)

Acrylic hose and funnels

Monochord (see appendix)

Cardboard guitars (see appendix)

Stethoscopes

Pots and pans

Spoons

The Setup

After presenting all the materials to kids, show them how to operate the stethoscope and monochord. This is another great activity to set up outside where the noise—or music—may not be as irritating to adult ears. Just make sure none of your neighbors are trying to sleep in late.

The Science

Amplitude, frequency, scale, and vibrations are all elements of sound that children may tune into as they play with sound making and sound sensing.

Real Life Science (ages 5–6)

Nathan's mother is a musician, so it's no wonder he began turning PVC pipe into instruments. A soda bottle funnel and a piece of pipe became an impressive horn. "Hello, hello, hello." Soon other children joined in and made a little megaphone music band. It was all discordant and loud and joyful. Though my ears suffered, the spontaneity and fun swept away my grown-up displeasure with what adults call a racket. They had invented megaphones.

Nalani picked up a pipe and started hitting one end of it with the palm of her hand. She tried another size and then another. Other children did the same. Katie said, "That made a different sound. I wonder why."

"It's shorter," Nalani answered matter-of-factly.

Children also shouted through the flexible tubes as though they where long shepherds' horns. Alex placed his horn against the classroom window and explained that he had created an invention that would make inside noise go out. Nick's "shouter, douter" was U-shaped with a funnel on either end.

Katie, Nick, and Ali took turns shouting and listening through it. Meanwhile, Josh sat listening, intense as a piano tuner, while he hit the monochord with a short section of pipe. Nearby, Katelyn and Leah were plucking at the cardboard guitars. "This is a birthday party!" Leah exclaimed.

"Quiet, I'm trying to listen" Matteo shouted. With a stethoscope plugged into his ears, he was listening to the window, to the garbage can, and to the air. Emmy listened to her belly and to her own voice and monitored a small animal burrow that Alex had discovered. Alex had been inside listening for sounds when he came back outside to announce, "I have an idea." Then, he dashed to the sand play area where he started "listening to the Earth." Then, he listened to the monochord as he plucked it. When Nick spoke into his stethoscope, he said, "This is like when the phone is against your ear and no one is talking."

Kid Science Library

Fiction

Baylor, Byrd. *Hawk I'm Your Brother.* New York: Scribner's, 1976.

A young boy who wants to fly like a hawk captures a bird and finally releases him. A good book to read after children have played with flying things.

Calhoun, Mary. *Hot Air Henry.* New York: Morrow, 1981.

Henry accidentally gets a ride on a hot-air balloon. Read this after kids have done some balloon play.

Livingston, Myra Cohn. *Up in the Air.* New York: Holiday, 1989.

A poetic impression of flight.

McGovern, Ann. *Too Much Noise.* Boston: Houghton Mifflin, 1967.

A man has a problem with too many sounds. If you read this while kids are exploring different sound makers, it may help them with describing some sounds that they make.

McKissack, Patricia C. *Mirandy and Brother Wind*. New York: Knopf, 1988.

Mirandy wants to win a dance contest and would like brother wind to be her partner. Read this during your windy day party!

Munsch, Robert. *Millicent and the Wind*. Scarborough, Ontario, Canada: Firefly Books, 1984.

A good book to accompany wind play.

Ross, Michael Elsohn. *Become a Bird and Fly*. Brookfield, CT: Millbrook Press, 1992.

Provide students with feathers to examine and binoculars to watch birds.

Showers, Paul. *The Listening Walk*. New York: Crowell, 1961.

Let kids take a listening walk. Bring along a tape recorder.

Seuss, Dr. *Mr. Brown Can Moo Can You?* New York: Random House, 1970.

Mr. Brown makes all kinds of wonderful sounds. Use this tale to tune children into the descriptive language of sounds.

Walter, Mildred Pitts. *Ty's One-Man Band*. New York: Four Winds, 1980.

A visitor in town teaches people to make musical instruments from all sorts of things. A good book to follow up sound play.

Nonfiction:

Barkan, Joanne. *Air, Air All Around*. Englewood Cliffs, NJ: Silver, 1990.

A simple introduction to the properties of air and its importance to living things.

Little, Kate. *Things That Fly*. London: Usborne, 1987.

A small, busy book packed with pictures of things that fly.

Overbeck, Cynthia. *How Seeds Travel*. Minneapolis, MN: Lerner, 1982.

An overview of seed dispersal.

Williams, Claudette, and David Evans. *Air and Flying*. New York: Dorling Kindserley, 1993.

One of the Let's Explore Science series. Plenty of pictures and questions.

Light

As connoisseurs of color and light, kids are constantly observing the details of shadows, light intensity, color variations, and reflections. Light intrigues the watchful eye, and kids take the time to watch. Young scientists equipped for exploring the daily light show will slowly unravel the way it works.

Lightworks

ages 3 & up

Light will sparkle and shine in the eyes of kids as they explore a variety of reflecting and refracting tools. Whether they compare the effects of each of the tools or create inventions from them, kids will illuminate the properties of light.

MATERIALS
Small Plexiglas or metal mirrors
Mylar or chrome tubes
Lucite or glass prisms
Tinfoil
Quartz and calcite crystals
Fresnel lenses
Marblescope or kaleidoscope
Convex/concave mirrors
Prism viewer
Spectroscopes
Small blocks for propping mirrors

The Setup

The greater the number of different materials provided, the more opportunities children will have to compare different aspects of light. Many of the materials above are inexpensive (see catalog list on page 190 for ordering information).

You can store all the materials in a tub. Discuss care of fragile items, such as prisms, before letting kids explore.

Outdoor exploration is ideal if you can monitor the use of the equipment to make sure items don't get lost.

The Science

The physics of light is not a lightweight topic, but kids will learn a lot by playing with it. They will investigate reflection (the bouncing of light rays) and refraction (the change in directions of light rays). Kids may also tumble into the color spectrum and stumble upon symmetry of the reflections. What did you see? How did that happen?

Real Life Science (ages 5–8)

"Everybody is a rainbow," Rico announced from behind a large prism.

"If you put tinfoil under the prism, it looks like the tinfoil is inside of it," instructed Nick.

"It's like a crystal," stated Ali.

Ideas and observations bounced at the speed of light from one child to another. Following Alex's lead, Katie created a mirror by molding a piece of tinfoil around one side of her prism. "I can see my eye," she announced.

Nick showed Alex how to use a mirror to reflect light onto the wall of the school. Rico watched and soon was shining light into people's faces; they quickly asked him to stop. Within a few minutes, most of the kids were making light patterns on the wall.

Lea watched and asked "How do you do that?" Then, she filled a small plastic container with grass and examined it through a prism. She told Katie, "Look, the grass is a rainbow."

Alex propped several mirrors against each other and noted that the sun reflected off them. Ali

watched and soon propped up several mirrors in the grass. Katie followed suit and said, "This is neat. I can reflect some stuff."

Now Alex had a mirror on top of a prism. "Look, you guys, a solar factory."

Nick and Alex lined several mirrors and a prism up to make a solar mousetrap. "See, when the mouse walks here, the prism reflects light in his eyes, and then the mirror will fall on him when he goes back."

In a short time, Nick and Alex had lined up fifteen mirrors side-by-side and had covered a plastic container with tinfoil.

"We are making a solar panel. The panels make electricity, and it gets stored in the tinfoil. The heat will stay in here," they told Carrol, who started propping up a series of his own mirrors.

Some children wandered about with prisms held up to their eyes. Leann invented reflection toss. Holding a mirror in front of her eyes, she explained to Allison. "Reflect light on my mirror and I'll reflect it back."

Color Goop

Children will massage, knead, and prod the bags of goop. They may discuss the merging of colors, the occurrence of bubbles, and other phenomena.

MATERIALS

I resealable freezer bag per kid
Cornstarch
Poster paints in primary colors
3 mixing bowls
Mixing spoons

The Setup

Pour two cups of water in each bowl. Mix in a little cornstarch at a time until you have goop the consistency of mustard. Add yellow paint to one bowl, blue to another, and red to the last. Blend well. Make a goop assortment pack by pouring different color combinations into the bags. Once you seal the bags tightly, they are ready to play with.

This kit is best at an indoor or outdoor table. Supply each child with a bag. If the kids want to play with the goop out of the bag, allow them to play outside where a making a mess would be OK.

The Science

Besides exploring a strange new texture, kids may observe how primary colors blend into secondary colors.

Real Life Science (ages 5–6)

Silently the children massaged the bags watching the colors merge and mix. After a little while, Karena announced, "It looks like a rainbow!" Holding her bag of yellow and red goop in the air, Claire asked the other kids, "What does red and yellow make?" No one answered. Claire looked at her bag some more and added, "It's cool."

Later, Claire noticed air bubbles in the bag. As she poked the bag, she observed, "It gets bigger and smaller and bigger. Hey, this little hole (bubble) goes backward."

All the other children continued to gently prod and push the bags. Colors continued to merge and mix, but no one said anything until Claire spoke up again when she reported her discovery.

"I know, red and yellow make orange." She pointed to her bag. "See the red and yellow are gone. It's orange."

Michelle replied, "I know what blue and yellow make. Green!"

As Claire pounded on her bag, she said, "This is slimy." Her bag was puffed out like a pillow. Karena asked how she made it do that and Claire showed her. "See, it's like making blood pressure."

Some of the bags began to leak onto the picnic table and the children excitedly discussed the goopy texture. When I noticed one child making a trail with the goop on the table, I steered him toward the sandy play area nearby. He trailed the goop all over the sand in intricate designs and other children joined him. A new investigation of goop had begun. Now they were examining how it disappeared in the sand and the texture of the new goop/sand mix. They noticed how it dried in long strands that were still partly sticky. After fifteen minutes, all of it—except for some that had dried on the asphalt and table—was gone and it was time for lunch.

Color Lab

Not only do colors get mixed during a session with droppers and colors, but observations swirl and combine to create a rich panorama of ideas.

MATERIALS
Poster paints or food coloring in primary colors

Styrofoam egg cartons or muffin tins

Mixing spoons

Droppers

3 bottle caps or small jar lids per kid

The Setup

Remove the lids from the egg cartons. Prepare water mixtures of each color in a separate plastic cup. The poster paint needs to be watered down until it has the consistency of ink. Give kids one capful of each primary color, one dropper, and one egg carton filled with water. Allow kids to replenish their water when they want to.

The Science

Mixing colors leads to investigations of solutions and primary colors.

Real Life Science (ages 5–7)

Was it an advanced university chemistry lab or an experimental art session? The scientists/artists carefully examined the changes as they added drops of color to an ever-changing mixture of pigments.

As Rhyen added drops of color his mix became darker and darker until it was black. Rico looked at Rhyen's cup and said, "I can make that, too."

When Ali asked Nick, "How did you make yours orange?" he gladly shared his recipe with her and she set to work making orange.

"I made purple," Emmy proudly pronounced.

"I really like purple," Ali said.

"Next time, I am going to make green," Emmy replied.

Nathan looked at his shirt and then his mix. "Look at this, now look at my tie-dyed shirt," he said to Rico.

Claire explained. "I know what makes green, blue and yellow." Then she set to work making green.

Karena looking at her pink mix and said, "Mine can be strawberry."

"Mine can be peach," replied Michelle.

On and on the children mixed. Some were so intrigued by the process that they remained silent. They just dripped and mixed and watched the changes.

Kid Science Library

Fiction

Asch, Frank. *Bear Shadow*. New York: Scholastic, 1990.
Another bear misadventure. Provide children with chalk so they can trace their shadows on blacktop or cement in the same spot several times during the day. Use different color of chalk each time.

Balian, Lorna. *A Garden for Groundhog*. Nashville, TN: Abingdon Press, 1985.
Make a paper groundhog and attach it to a stick. Place it outside and let kids observe its shadow. Provide materials to trace shadow.

Jonas, Ann. *Color Dance*. New York: Greenwillow, 1989.
Three girls do a color mixing dance with scarves.

Jonas, Ann. *Reflections*. New York: Greenwillow, 1987.
A book to read twice, up and down. Read after exploring reflections.

Nonfiction

Jeunesse, Gallimard. *Colors, A First Discovery Book*. New York: Scholastic, 1991.
This book uses attractive art and see-through pages to introduce kids to colors and color mixing.

Jeunesse, Gallimard. *Light, A First Discovery Book*. New York: Scholastic, 1992.
Rich graphics and transparencies are used to introduce light topics from shadows to fireflies.

Mcloughlin Bros. *The Magic Mirror, an Antique Optical Toy*. New York: Dover, 1979.

Taylor, Kim. *Light*. New York: Wiley, 1988.
A flying-start science book of facts and directed experiments.

Mechanics

Kids' enthusiasm for machinery can become infectious. Parents and teachers of young children may find themselves examining big rigs, cranes, and dozers with a more critical eye. They may catch themselves wondering how a TV works or how a modem sends those messages. Machines that didn't exist in our youth are the result of applying the amazing scientific discoveries of the past few decades. Though simple to operate, their workings remain mysterious. Exploring machines eventually—after a doctorate or two—leads to an understanding of how they work.

Since modern society produces machinery with planned obsolescence in mind, complex mechanisms and their fascinating components soon become trash. These discards are free toys for curious kids. As your passion for technology grows, don't be surprised if you become an avid collector of technological effluvia, too.

Disassembly Line

Is it the **RCA** factory on a very bad day or is it the how-does-it-work detectives in the heart of an investigation? **Give kids some tools and a variety of broken gadgets and you will witness things coming apart at a rapid rate. As kids disassemble equipment, they will share theories on why it broke, explain what it's made of, and make plans for its future use.**

The Setup

It may be helpful for children—especially the younger ones—to pre-loosen screws for them. A quick demonstration will provide kids with the basic idea of how to use the tools, but be ready to intervene if you observe unsafe tool use.

MATERIALS

4 sizes of Phillips head and flathead screwdrivers

Pliers

Containers for children to put small parts in

VCRs, CBs, cassette players, toasters, waffle irons, old clocks, and TVs (with the screens removed) from a dump, repair shop, parent, friend, or thrift store

Retrieve motors before they are damaged. VCRs, tape players, and disc players have motors to turn things, and you can use them for future explorations. If possible, keep the motors connected to pulley or gear mechanisms.

What did you find? What does it do? Why do you think the machine stopped working?

The Science

This is a true investigation of the science behind technology. Kids will wonder how things work and what different parts are for. Dismantling appliances is a great introduction to electrical circuits, pulleys, springs, levers, magnets, and other components that we use every day. Kids learn to use a variety of tools and gain much practice in sharing scientific equipment.

Real Life Science (ages 5–8)

The kids dismantled with vigor, anticipating hidden treasures. A VCR is a treasure chest of colorful wires, precious circuit boards, pulleys, magnets, gears, and other intriguing gizmos. There were enough screws to give all the kids ample practice removing them. After an hour, the kids were impressed by their initial booty. After three days, there was a mass of wonderful parts to play with. Interest was high. Everyone wanted to take things apart. Luckily, we had not only a VCR, but a cassette player and a CB radio.

Some kids patiently unscrewed, methodically cut wires, and carefully separated components. Others hammered with everything on everything. Things came apart. What looked like serious destruction was also serious exploration. Kids fiddled with gears, buttons, and springs to discover how stuff worked. One kid discovered the spring that made the door to the cassette player swing open and another child ran around displaying a magnet he had discovered. A girl excitedly showed her coworkers the little "paints" (transistors) on the circuit board.

Some children were troubleshooters par excellence.

"This is why it didn't work—the battery wasn't charged," explained Amanda as she held up a capacitor.

"I know why it didn't work," announced Ricky as he pointed to a resister, "It's burnt."

"We cut all these [wires] so we wouldn't get shocked."

Leann pointed to a pile of screws that she had unscrewed and exclaimed, "Look at all these nails here."

Other kids knew what circuit boards were. They all learned new terms by listening to each other. Nick exclaimed, "Alex, let's pretend we are wire guys, rr-boing-rrr!" Rico pointed at the letters on the VCR controls and informed us, "I'll take off the ABCs."

They continued to take apart more ABCs and everything else for months.

Electrotorium

Chances are that, if you hand children batteries and motors, they'll figure out how to make something work. Motors may spin and whiz. Pulleys may drive gears. Bells may even go off. The battery holder was clipped to circuit boards, gears, and even casings.

Some kids found motors and clipped on the wires. Eventually, they discovered that the motors worked when they connected the black wires to black and the red to red.

MATERIALS

Battery holders (for C or D cells)

Batteries (C or D)

Small alligator clips

Electrical tape

Motors from gadgets that kids have taken apart (see Disassembly Line, page 91)

Other parts from gadgets

The Setup

Purchase battery holders and small motors at stores such as Radio Shack or from the catalogs listed on page 192. You can also collect motors from electronic gadgets that kids may have taken apart.

Attach alligator clips to the ends of battery holder wires. Secure the connection with electrical tape. Place batteries in battery holder in positions indicated.

Demonstrate when you connect batteries to a motor. Disconnect the batteries and motor before letting kids try it for themselves. At some point, discuss what is safe electrical play and what isn't. Emphasize that kids should not play with electrical outlets or any large machines or appliances.

The Science

Polarity, complete circuits, and electrical storage are some of the properties of electricity that kids may investigate as they play with motors and batteries. Surrounded with gadgets and batteries, children will develop experience with electricity at an early age. As they play with motors, they will further their understanding of how electricity makes machines work.

Real Life Science (ages 5–6)

Within seconds, Claire had discovered how to make the wheels from a dismantled battery-powered car move. When nothing happened after she connected the battery clips to the motor, she switched the position of the clips and looked supremely pleased as the wheels spun. Next, she hooked up the clips to another motor from an old tape recorder and watched as it moved a pulley.

"It hot!" she commented to Matteo as she held forth an alligator clip for him to feel. Matteo had just finished taking apart an old answering machine and had asked Claire for the batteries so he could "make it go." Using Claire's batteries, he tried to make the motor in the answering machine move. He connected the clips to several different sets of loose wires in the gutted machine, but nothing happened.

"The batteries are out," commented Matteo.

"No, they aren't because I hooked them up and it went in circles," said Claire pointing to the tape recorder motor.

"It works!" Matteo exclaimed when Claire reconnected the batteries to her motor.

Back at his answering machine, Matteo continued trying to get the motor going but moved to another activity when nothing happened.

"This is neat," Timmy commented to no one in particular as he set the car wheels spinning. He asked Eddie, "Anyone want to see what this does?" Eddie ignored him as he intently worked on another project. When Timmy left the batteries behind, Kyle soon discovered them. Quietly, Kyle observed the effects of connecting and disconnecting a single clip. He continued this exploration for awhile before trying to drive the wheels across the floor.

Gears

Plastic gear sets encourage experimentation. Children will readily arrange the gears in a variety of ways and may use the resulting creations in imaginative play about operating machines of various sorts.

MATERIALS

Gears (for free gears, salvage the guts from VCRs, tape decks, and clocks or for sources of gear toys see appendix)

Egg beaters, clock works, can openers, and other common pieces of equipment with gears

The Setup

Place the gears and other equipment on a table or another level surface.

The Science

Gears not only transfer motion, but they can change its rate or direction. Bicycles, tape players, watches, and even egg beaters employ gears to regulate movement of parts. Playing with gears can lead to a greater understanding of how these machines work.

Real Life Science (ages 2–7)

Karena and Michelle assembled the plastic gears into several different working configurations. When Alex interlocked all his gears in a close arrangement, nothing happened. They were locked in place. Alex muttered to himself, "Nothing happened, must be too many gears." When Rico ventured over to take a look, Alex told him, "If I had a few more of these, I could make a chairlift." He was remembering the big pulleys and gears at the ski resort where his father worked.

Rico rummaged through a box of electronic guts from a VCR and tape deck, fished out a small set of gears, and noticed that it was connected to the motor by an axle.

At the preschool, two-year-old Langston quietly explored the gears. He spinned them and changed their positions. For half an hour, four-year-old Johnny constructed a complex system of gears as other children came and went.

Pulleys & Buckets

ages 4 & up

Pulleys and buckets inspire experiments in lifting and moving objects. Kids will include the pulleys in imaginative activities or they may just playfully pull.

MATERIALS
Small pulleys

6-inch piece of cord for each pulley

10-foot length of venetian blind cord for each pulley

1-foot length of cord for each pulley

S hook for each pulley

Plastic buckets of various sizes

The Setup

Use the 6-inch cords to tie the pulleys to playground overhead bars or low tree branches. Thread the cord through the pulleys and tie the S hook to one end. Show kids the buckets and let them choose the cargo.

The Science

It's physics again! Wheels aren't just for cars. Pulleys have wheels, too. Wheels decrease friction and make movement easier. Children will investigate loads, friction, and force.

Real Life Science (ages 5–8)

Buckets were filled with sand, water, toys, and other objects. "1,2,3, pull."

As buckets went up and down, kids compared the loads. Leann, Jennifer, and Amanda filled a large bucket with sand and hoisted it like sailors raising a mainsail. Heave ho. Children worked in twos, threes, and even fours with particularly challenging cargo.

Many of the kids were deeply engaged in imaginative play.

"Alex, lets pretend we are making an invention," said Nick.

"OK."

Lea came over and helped Alex fill a bucket with sand.

"Now," said Alex, and Nick pulled on the other end of the cord raising the bucket.

"Let's pretend we are digging a mine," said Alex.

"OK," agreed Leah and Nick.

Pulley Board

Children will hoist the bar upward by themselves or in pairs. At first, just lifting the bar itself will be a challenge, but later kids may try lifting cups of water, sand, or other objects.

MATERIALS

1 pulley board (see appendix)

Plastic cups, toys, and other lightweight unbreakable objects

The Setup

Mount this apparatus to a bar or fence corner. Secure it with string.

Before letting kids use the pulley board, elicit ideas about how to use it safely. For example, it is dangerous to stand under or near the board. Let kids know that it is also not safe to stand on the board. Monitor the kids during their initial use.

The Science

This activity is problem solving at its finest. It takes communication and coordination of minds and bodies. There's physics here, too. Applying equal force and speed is the secret to keeping the board level. Add cups of water and observing levelness gets really fun.

Real Life Science (ages 5–8)

"Pull, more, more, hold."

Allison and Nick tried to raise Nick's lunchbox to the top. It slid off, but they tried again and again. Eventually they mastered the right tension and pace, and up it rose like a window washer's scaffold. Next came a bucket of water. Then a bucket of sand. Then three cups of water. Then five. Allison gave it a try by herself. Then Nick followed suit.

"Stop, pull, now, slower, faster." Each pair of kids that raised the board carried on their own directional dialogue while they lifted their loads skyward.

Ramps

Rolling a ball down a ramp is fun. Rolling a ball down a flexible ramp is even more exciting. These urethane ramps made from pipe insulation lend themselves to an endless array of experiments. Kids will discover that they can place the ramps end to end, alongside one another, over and under, and in all kinds of other ingenious configurations. Playing with ramps not only leads to new experiences with the physics of falling but encourages cooperative discovery. On top of all this, only a minor investment of time and money is required to get things rolling.

MATERIALS

One pack foam pipe insulation (3-foot sections used for one ¼-inch copper pipe)

Bag of marbles (dozen or more)

Plastic cups or 8-ounce yogurt containers

Micro-cars

Blocks

Milk crates

The Setup

Use a sharp knife to slice the foam length-wise in half. This is an active and sometimes noisy activity, so keep this in mind when you decide whether to set it up inside or outdoors.

The Science

Kids may not know it, but they are exploring gravity, friction, energy, engineering, and lots more. As they work together, perhaps they may even become conscious of the marvelous synergy of collaborative inventing.

Real Life Science (ages 5–8)

Ali made a ramp by leaning the insulation on a bench. She placed a car on it, but it didn't roll. "My car is too big." She drove the car down the ramp with her hand. Later, she got a smaller car and then a marble. Soon Nalani was helping her engineer a long ramp supported in the middle by a milk crate, blocks, and a lunch box.

Other children were racing things. "Which marble will go faster? Will a car beat a marble?" Rico set up his ramp so the marble would drop into a cup. Leah and Katelyn placed cups on the end of their ramps.

Nick leaned his ramp against a shelf and placed the cup at the bottom.

"Look," he predicted to Rhyen, "it's going to knock the cup up." The cup moved back when it was hit. Nick moved it several times and then rolled a marble into it. Each time, it moved back but not up.

Ricky rolled a car down his ramp, and it stalled at the end. When he rolled a marble down, it bounced the car off the ramp. Ricky re-created this crash scene many times and each time it was accompanied by sound effects.

Allison arrived and immediately made her ramp into a U shape. With one end tucked under her chin, she rolled a marble and watched it roll back and forth. Next, she twisted the insulation and tried to roll a marble down it. Later she discovered she could use the back of the chair to keep it curved.

Amanda, Leann, and Elizabeth made a ramp supported by chairs and then created an overpass by placing another ramp above and perpendicular to it. Later, others joined them and helped them make a series of ramps supported by chairs that emptied the rolling marbles into a crate.

After the ramps had been in class for several weeks, I noticed Maira had set up a U shaped ramp between two chairs. In it she had placed seven or eight marbles. She rolled one marble down the ramp. When it struck the row of marbles, the marble furthest away moved. For over half an hour, Maira rolled one marble at a time and intensely observed this fascinating transfer of force.

Spin Play

With tops, a turntable, and a gyro-scope, many children will soon begin to notice the similarities and differ-ences between the movements of the different objects. Kids may also inves-tigate how colors of spinning objects blend. These experiences can lead to the development of grand theories on spinning movement, as well as more creative experimentation.

MATERIALS
Old record turntable

Tops

Gyroscope

Small toys and bottle tops

The Setup

Review how to operate the different tools. By suggesting that kids change the speed slowly, you may extend the longevity of the turntable. You also can tape the arm down so that it can't be played with. You can use turntables with broken motors by simply spinning them with hand power.

The Science

Speed and mass affect the way spinning objects respond to gravity. Explorations with a variety of objects may lead to observations about these relationships.

Real Life Science (ages 5–7)

Things were spinning. The old record player went around and around and around. Alex placed his fingers on it and dreamily felt it spin. Ali and Rico experimented making sounds by letting their fingers and other objects run against the top and sides. Nick dropped an unsharpened pencil onto the revolving surface and Rico suggested, "Put it on full blast. Watch it spin off."

His prediction was confirmed when the increased speed sent the pencil on a trip. Again they tested the staying power of the pencil as they watched it spin at different speeds. At slow speed the pencil stayed on. Josh wandered over to watch and commented, "It works." When the speed was increased to 45, Rico asked Nick, "What's it gonna do? It might hit you, it might not." When the pencil finally shot off, Nick observed, "It doesn't want to go around. It wants to go straight, so it shoots off."

Next the boys found some tops and spun them on the surface of the turntable. The tops flew off the outer edge. When they placed them right near the center in the slight depression, they not only stayed but appeared to the boys to be spinning. With the stems of the tops resting against the post in the middle of the turntable, the tops indeed seemed to spin of their own accord.

"How does it do that?" asked Rico.

"Gravity," Alex answered matter-of-factly.

Later, they added an eraser. The boys pretended that the eraser was a shark trying to catch two tops that were people.

Meanwhile, Katie and Rhyen explored the gyroscope with zeal. Both of them needed adult assistance to get it going, but were soon helping each other master its operation.

Pendulums

Pendulums invite swinging. Children will push, pat, kick, or simply drop objects into swinging motion. Using toys as weights can evolve into episodes of imaginative play. Repetitive swinging may accidentally jump into experiments with side and circular swinging. Using a variety of different size objects may lead to observation on how mass effects the force or breadth of a swing.

MATERIALS
String

Paper clips

PVC pipe stands (see appendix)

Sock stuffed with soft material (optional)

Blocks, milk cartons, or other objects that can be knocked over (optional)

The Setup

Make stands using the PVC pipe (see appendix). Attach one string to the pipe stands, a bar, a branch, or another suitable object under which a pendulum can freely swing. Tie a paper clip to the end of the string, or attach a ring magnet, toy, stuffed sock, or another object as a weight.

For variation, attach a weighted string to a wall or bulletin board to create a pendulum that moves back and forth along a vertical surface.

The Science

Pendulums, though deceptively simple, hold the key to understanding basic physical laws. Most kids begin their lives rocking back and forth in swinging cradles. When they are old enough, they graduate to swing sets. Each experience with swinging objects leads to a deeper understanding of the relationships between force, gravity, and friction.

Real Life Science (ages 2–7)

Two pendulums were attached to one bar. After letting them both go at the same time, David watched them swing together back and forth, back and forth. Michelle, on the other hand, let each of hers go at separate times and watched intently, totally oblivious to the nonstop chatter around her. Alex placed two ring magnets at the end of each pendulum and set them swinging. When he tried to sit on this miniature swing, it fell apart. Karena watched this swinging play from afar. In her hand, she had a string of beads that she swayed back and forth.

Two-year-old Jessica investigated a pendulum for almost an hour. Part of the time she swung a little car back and forth to her friend Hannah, but most of the time operated it alone. With pushes, taps, slaps, and even kicks, she set the car into swinging motion. All the while she commented to herself, "Whoa, it go backwards, it swing, whoa."

When she set the car swinging in a circular motion, her whole head rotated as she followed the movement. Nearby, Alex was swinging two little toy spacemen on his pendulum and pretending they were on an adventure in space. As he watched them swing back and forth, he chanted, "Tic toc, tic toc, tic toc."

Swinging Buckets

ages 2 & up

The bucket will swing back and forth as kids examine the movement of the flowing water. Place it on the black-top, and kids might notice the patterns made by the dripping water. Or place it on the sand, and they might examine erosion. On a lawn, the bucket acts as a simple watering device.

MATERIALS
Quart-sized plastic containers
Large tub of water
String
Large paper clips or O rings
PVC pipe stands (see appendix)

The Setup

Make a bucket by poking holes on opposite sides of the container approximately half an inch from the lip. Cut an 18-inch piece of string. Insert a paper clip or O ring in each hole and tie a piece of string to one side. Loop the other end of the string over the crosspiece of the PVC pipe stand, and then connect it to the other side of the bucket. Do this for each bucket.

Cut a third hole the diameter of a pencil or smaller in the bottom of each container. The water will drip out this hole.

Start with a small hole and enlarge it if water doesn't flow out fast enough for kids to notice.

Set up outside on the lawn, blacktop, or sand play area.

The Science

Watching water flow out of the swinging buckets provides kids with the opportunity to track the variety of movements made by swinging objects.

Real Life Science (ages 2–5)

Sean and Timmy traveled back and forth to and from the water tub scooping water for the pendulum buckets. After pouring it in, they set the buckets in motion and stood by to observe them swing. Each time, they silently watched until the buckets were empty.

"It makes a good sprinkler," Alex observed as he passed by.

After watching Sean and Timmy, Billy and Logan started working with another pendulum. As three-year-old Logan pushed the bucket, the string slid along the top of the stand, and the bucket collided with one of the posts. After swings were halted several times by the post, Logan purposefully moved the string to the middle of the crosspiece and the swinging continued unimpaired.

Plumbline Hats

Plumblines lead children to explore the notion of straightness, the movement of pendulums, and the effects of head or whole body movement. Some children may wear the hats for a long time and others will discard them after a quick exploration.

MATERIALS
Adjustable baseball caps

Clothespins

18-inch pieces of string

Weights, such as large washers, nuts, or small plastic figures

The Setup

Attach one end of the string to the hat brim with a clothespin, and tie a weight to the other end. Adjust the hat to fit the child's head, and adjust the length of the string so that the weight hangs near his or her chest. Ask children if they have ever seen anyone use a plumbline and discuss what plumblines are used for.

The Science

A plumbline is an instrument used to determine the true vertical. In other words, it shows the straight path that heavy objects will fall to earth. As children fool about with this tool, they will explore the idea of straight up and down as they compare the plumbline with other objects. Is the wall, the tree, or my friend straight? The plumbline is also a pendulum and, like all pendulums, will come to rest at the lowest point.

Real Life Science (ages 5–8)

As Zachary encountered people on his tour around the room, he stopped and stood next to them before lining them up with the plumbline. After a moment, he announced, "You're straight." After observing Zachary, Nalani and Emily repeated his procedure. "Do me," requested Denise.

Josh put on two hats and swung his head back and forth trying to make the two plumblines come together.

Kid Science Library

Fiction

Lionni, Leo. *Pezzitino.* New York: Pantheon, 1975.

A story about a little square who thinks it's a part of something bigger that has fallen apart. What it discovers is that it is made of its own little pieces.

Ross, Michael. *What Makes Everything Go?* El Portal, CA: Yosemite Association, 1979.

An alligator explains energy.

Nonfiction

Berger, Melvin. *Telephones, Televisions, and Toilets. How They Work and What Can Go Wrong.* Nashville, TN: Ideals, 1993.

A colorful description of the workings of everyday machines.

Gibbons, Gail. *Tool Book.* New York: Holiday, 1982.

Text and bright, colorful illustrations introduce the purposes and uses of basic tools.

Rockwell, Anne and Harlow. *Machines.* New York: MacMillan, 1972.

A clear introduction to machines and mechanical concepts.

Rockwell, Anne and Harlow. *The Toolbox.* New York: MacMillan, 1971.

Simple text describes the uses of the tools in a toolbox.

Building

Bees build hives, gophers construct burrows, and kids will build most anything at all. As creatures living in complex edifices, it's no wonder that our offspring are builders from the start. As they mimic our sophisticated structures, kids learn about load, balance, gravity, the suitability of materials, and a score of other concepts that will prepare them for careers as engineers, architects, or homeowners. Providing a rich array of materials and circumstances may lead to marvels in kid construction and social organization. Recording these temporary achievements with snapshots can be helpful in preserving the experience.

Measuring

Past experience in observing adults using measuring tools will provide children with the vague ideas about how to play with each tool. Use of tools in imaginative play will allow kids to construct their own concepts of measurement.

MATERIALS
Balances and bathroom scales
Measuring tapes and rulers
Compasses
Hourglasses and cooking timers
Meat, soil, air thermometers
Unifix cubes
Measuring cups

The Setup

Collect tools that are kid-safe, such as plastic compasses, hourglasses, and thermometers instead of glass ones. Ask the kids for ideas about how the tools work and how to use them safely.

The Science

What time is it? How fast are we going? How big is it? Kids ask these questions long before they are capable of understanding how to measure time, speed, or size. As with language, they grow to understand the concept of measuring things by being immersed in an environment where measuring occurs. Children construct their own ideas about time, volume, and weight and only become proficient when they are developmentally ready. Measurement is a major aspect of scientific exploration and playing with the tools of measurement one more important activity of kid scientists at play.

What can you do with that tool? What can you find out with it?

Real Life Science (ages 5–8)

Alex walked around with a thermometer in his hand and proclaimed, "It's getting warmer each step I take."

"I'm going to see," said Nick with his thermometer at hand. "We are testing how hot the bicycles are," Alex stated as he placed his thermometer near each bike parked in the rack.

"Hot, hot, hot, cold, hot," Ricky announced as he wandered about the yard.

As Leann walked in a zigzag line holding a compass in her palm, she told Allison, "I'm following the compass, it's telling me where to go. It tells me where the gold is."

Meanwhile, Jennifer, equipped with a level, silently checked shelves, picnic tables, and the warped surface of the blacktop.

"It's this big," other children announced as they measured the length of tables, chairs, and toys. Not being able to read the numbers didn't stop them from investigating size. The same was true with scales, thermometers, and measuring cups. With a basic idea of how tools work, the kids checked out the neighborhood.

Junk Inventions

ages 4 & up

It's easy to imagine the wild and ingenious inventions that kids will create when given a diverse set of materials. Some may build without a purpose in mind. Later when they examine their spontaneous inventions, they may invent a use for them. Others may concoct devices with a clear goal in mind but diverge from their plans as they become intrigued by new possibilities. Whether they are quiet tinkerers or nonstop idea people, wonderful fantasies will bloom from their inventive minds.

MATERIALS

Masking tape

Plastic-bag ties

Selected parts from Disassembly Line (page 91)

Broken toys and other small junk parts

Natural objects, such as twigs, shells, and acorns

Bits of string or yarn

Toolbox (see appendix)

The Setup

When you set out the leftover parts from the Disassembly Line kit, be sure to exclude any with sharp ends or jagged edges. Put the junk in a tub. Let the kids know that they can make whatever they want with the materials.

The Science

Even though their inventions might never work in reality, kids are able to imagine how a variety of components might work together to solve a problem or create a tool. Devising technological solutions to problems, even when they are just pretend, requires a complex level of scientific thought. Inventions are often the true test of a scientist's ability to transform observation into active application.

Real Life Science (ages 5–8)

Ever since their teacher had read the story of the escaped gingerbread man and had shown them the wanted posters, the kids had been on the lookout. During recess they had dug pit traps in the sandbox and shared many ideas about how to capture the fugitive cookie.

After they were invited to play with the junk box, the kids' thoughts immediately settled on their doughy hunt. Zack attached an antenna and circuit board to part of an old clock and notified his fellow inventors that he was creating an alarm that would alert them of the G-man's presence. Rhyen assisted him in this endeavor by adding a wheel. If the G-man touched the wheel Rhyen said he would get spun into a trip wire that then set off the alarm. Meanwhile, Alex had made a seat that would flip over when the cookie guy sat on it, and David made another type of tripper trap. Despite the predominant interest in traps, not all the children were thinking of the escaped cookie. During all the excited brainstorming, Katie quietly fashioned bracelets and a necklace from the electronic waste.

Straw Construction

The ease with which straws connect with clay is an invitation to build, rebuild, and imagine. Without any hesitation, children will transmogrify the inanimate clay and straws into whatever the ever-changing assemblages suggest.

MATERIALS
Modeling clay
Drinking straws

The Setup

Cut the straws in half to make shorter lengths. Set both the clay and straws on a table and let the kids go at it. Kids may add toys or other objects to the play. Since particles of clay may stick to the objects, you may want to monitor what they use.

The Science

As children attempt to create different combinations of clay and straws, they will inevitably be challenged to solve problems. As they gain more experience with the materials, they may make predictions and test them. They will likely create models of real or imaginary things, and some children may even collaborate.

Real Life Science (ages 2–4)

When Hannah stuck a piece of clay on either end of a straw, Josh commented, "They could be hammers."

After Brook poked a dozen or so straws into a chunk of clay, he announced, "I made an Indian house."

"I made a spider," said Alec, holding up a clay spider with three straw legs.

Without any suggestions the kids created a series of models. The older children shared their creations and embarked on new creations as they discovered what their friends were doing.

On the other hand, two-year-old Ellie worked in silent concentration. She was obviously watching the older children. Like Alec and Seth, she made a spider that she walked along the tabletop. When she set it legs down, it stood for a moment before toppling over and losing its appendages. Ellie merely smiled and began putting it back together.

Later, Ellie began to arrange straws in geometric patterns that reached into Nikita's space next door. Nikita knocked them out of the way, but Ellie just rearranged them without any comment. Nikita was trying to make a straw tower by placing the end of one straw on the top of another. Without clay connecting the straws, it toppled over. Next, she tried to stand a straw on the ends of two straws embedded in a base of clay, but that fell down too. Next to her, Ellie now was connecting straws and clay together to make a long horizontal chain. She had discovered what Nikita needed to know to solve her problem, but Nikita didn't notice. Perhaps another day the ideas of both girls would merge and a tower would rise from the synthesis.

Shelters

The process of kid construction is definitely not linear. Blocks go up only to come down minutes later. Entire walls may be pilfered from adjacent home sites. Plans can be made and remade. Despite collapsed ceilings or one-foot-high doors, kids make themselves comfortable in their homemade shelters. Besides homes, kids also construct roles for themselves. Whole families, towns, and even neighborhoods with pets included may rise from their imaginations.

MATERIALS

Large blocks

Boxes

PVC pipe

PVC pipe stands (see appendix)

Milk crates

Cardboard tubes

Clear sheets of Plexiglas

Sheets of cardboard

Old bed sheets

Large cardboard boxes

The Setup

Place the materials outside on a lawn or blacktop or inside in a corner of a room.

Set out all the materials and review their safe use. Kids may occasionally seek your assistance for a specific task. It's OK to lend a hand, but try to let them do the problem solving.

The Science

From figuring out how to keep the walls from careening down to laying the roof, kids become immersed in solving problems. Balance and load are constantly tested. Spatial relationships are explored. Ideas evolve into less lofty realities as children learn the limits of their materials. Besides structures, kids will build cooperatively out of the need for more hands and thoughts. Like other applied sciences, construction is a real-life challenge.

Real Life Science (ages 5–6)

Karena happily surveyed the wreckage of Claire's discarded shelter and began humming. Here and there she went gathering blocks. On one of her excursions she acquired a stray cat (Eddie). He curiously followed her around meowing as she stacked blocks to make walls. One wall and then another rose up, and soon Karena was ready to transform a sheet into a roof. Each time she threw the sheet up, down it came again. "Oh no," she muttered with the fallen sheet in her hand.

Looking at the kitty, she asked quite earnestly, "Eddie, can you help me?" Eddie immediately ceased being a kitty and began assisting Karena. Claire, seeing her home revived, joined them to secure the roof from the gusts that had demolished the house before.

After they placed blocks around the bottom edges, Eddie crawled inside. Claire asked, "Where am I gonna sleep?"

Karena replied, "With Eddie."

"No way," said Claire, and she left.

As Karena adjusted walls, a screaming gust blew down one whole side. Karena wandered off while Eddie remained inside the partially collapsed house, contented to be a curled-up kitty.

Kid Science Library

Fiction

McClerran, Alice. *Roxaboxen*. New York: Scholastic, 1991.

Children create their own play town near small a desert town. Let kids build a community using sheets, boxes, rocks, sticks, and other everyday materials.

Myller, Rolf. *How Big is a Foot?* New York: Dell, 1990.

The king wants to give his wife a bed, but has a problem deciding how big it should be. Use this book as an introduction to standard measurement.

Schotter, Roni. *Captain Snap and the Children of Vinegar Lane*. Boston: Joy Street, 1988.

Captain Snap makes wonderful things from junk and lets the children help. Read this before letting kids make junk inventions.

Nonfiction

Garrison, Webb. *Why Didn't I Think of That? From Alarm Clocks to Zippers*. Englewood Cliffs, NJ: Prentice, 1977.

A book about inventions and the inspirations that led to them.

McCauley, David. *The Way Things Work*. Boston: Houghton Mifflin, 1988.

An incredibly detailed book about mechanical things. Children ages 5 and up will want to know what everything is and how it works.

Williams, Claudette and David Evans. *Building Things*. New York: Dorling Kindserley, 1993.

One of the Let's Explore Science series. Includes plenty of pictures and questions.

Little Critters

Seven

Ahh!! How cute! EEEK!!

Animals capture the hearts and souls of young people. Whether in fear or friendship, strong emotions develop for the other creatures that share our planet. By a young age, many children have had extensive experience with small backyard critters while others have not, whether it's due to lack of opportunity or, worse yet, reluctance. A child frightened by a dog may avoid other mammals. A child warned about spiders and other bugs may shy away from all crawly critters. When kids can watch other children joyfully and safely explore small critters, they are apt to abandon fears and get swept away by fascination.

Along with learning how to treat their peers, kids can learn to respect other living things. Through positive role modeling, stories, and extensive play, children can form empathy for fellow animals. In a society that is often violent, learning to love living things is the first step in developing a greater life ethic. Share your love of living things and rescue those little creatures from intentional or unintentional harm whenever it's necessary. As kids emulate your respectful attitude, they'll guide their younger colleagues.

Another respectful role to play is that of the patron of questions. Record questions that you overhear or those that the kids ask you directly. These recorded questions can then become the paths children take into adult-supported experimentation or research. "Does a snail have eyes?" can lead to observation, experiments with vision, or reading a book about snails.

to Get

...wns or gardens by find-
... soil called castings.
...oil and mucus mixture
...rom their burrows. At a
...like small plugs of soil, but
...esemble brown toothpaste
... a tube. Dig wherever you
...nd worms should be nearby.
...d colder the soil, the deeper
...rrow. If you can't dig up your
...s, purchase some from a bait
...sery, or neighborhood worm

Care & Feeding

A liter soda bottle with the narrowed section cut off makes a fine worm motel. Just
fill the container halfway with moist soil,
add a handful of damp dead tree leaves, and
drop the worms in. Place an old sock over
the top and keep the container in a cool
dark place.

The Science

Watch for investigations of worm senses,
locomotion, and other behaviors. Children
will have many questions that you can
record for later discussion.

What does your worm do? Why?
What else do you know about worms?

Animals to Watch

Though most backyard creatures are
harmless, there are some that can inflict
painful bites or stings. Developing an
awareness of these critters will provide
kids with the information they need to dis-
criminate between the animals that are
touchable and those that are not.
Prominent displays of these animals at
home or in the classroom will enable children to identify them in the field. Be sure
to keep all containers out of reach of children when adults are not present.

Stress the importance of leaving these
creatures alone if kids encounter them
outdoors. Try to instill a respect for the
self-defense abilities of these animals, without inspiring too much fear of animals in
general.

Black Widow Spiders Black widows are
relatively non-aggressive animals, but they
will bite when bothered by probing hands.
Unfortunately, they like to build their webs
in crevices, corners, and other out-of-the-
way places that kids sometimes explore.
Only the female is poisonous, and she usually hides herself at the bottom of her dis-
tinctive cobweb. Children can easily learn
to recognize this telltale web when a black
widow and her web are displayed in a terrarium or large gallon jar. Since most spiders can live for days without food or
water, it is not necessary to feed your spider guest if it stays for a week or less.

Scorpions The further north you live, the
less venomous these creatures become.
Like spiders, they will only sting when they
feel threatened. Keep them in a glass jar
and provide an object, such as a rock or
toy car, for them to crawl under.

Centipedes Most centipedes living in
North America have a relatively weak
venom, even so their sting can be painful. A
jar with the bottom covered with moist
topsoil or leaf litter will provide them with
comfortable quarters.

Earthworms

ages 2 & up

Earthworms are simple, fail-safe creatures to explore. Though worms are seemingly void of personality, kids readily include them in imaginative play. They become babies that need a bath or a family living in the dirt. As children play with worms they'll notice new things about earthworm bodies and behavior. Some children will hold them endlessly, while others will watch and only occasionally give the wigglers a gentle nudge.

Worms are practical, as well as plentiful. They are common residents of lawns and gardens, as well as typical bait shop fare. Worms are a gift to gardeners, both young and old. While experienced gardeners appreciate them for their soil improvement services, young gardeners will almost immediately classify them as fascinating critters that don't run away.

MATERIALS

Worms (the more the better)

One or more plastic tubs containing an inch of water

Watercolor brushes

Moist washcloths or paper towels

Magnifying lenses

Large leaves

Place materials at a table or on a lawn. Share ideas about how to be gentle worm friends. Give one worm to each child who wants one.

Where
Locate worms in law
ing small piles
Castings are a s
worms cast out
glance, they look
up close they
squeezed from
find castings a
The drier an
they will bu
own worm
shop, nur
catcher.

Real Life Science (ages 2–5)

Two two-year-olds, Claire and Denise, were squealing as they looked at the worms. Claire called them snakes. Denise backed up and watched from afar. She did not want to touch the worms. I sat quietly and watched, only intervening to protect a worm or magnifying lens from damage.

Eddie poked at his worm with his lens, and soon two pieces of worm were wiggling around on the table. I was concerned for the worms' lives, so I gently intervened and showed him how to look through the lens. He continued to use the lens for a poker. On behalf of the worms, I refocused him by trading a brush for the lens. The brush was gentler on the worms.

Sean touched and observed his worm intently. Though he was often rough with the other children, he was surprisingly gentle with his worm. The children busily played, observed, and talked.

"If you put it on the table, it will fall down."

"He's on the chair."

"It pooped."

After twenty minutes, most of the children gravitated toward other activities, but Sean and Claire continued to examine the worms. Claire attempted to pick up her worm and wanted help. I suggested that Sean help her. Claire yakked at her worm as she played with it.

"I hate worms," she said, "Scary. The snake bit my finger."

Despite her words, she was mesmerized by the silent, slippery creature.

As I put the worms away, I examined them for damage. Besides Eddie's worm, two other worms had lost part of their tail segments, which they would likely grow back. These worms, like martyrs to public service, had not been damaged in vain. The children were learning to like worms and would, with luck, continue loving them for a lifetime.

Snails

ages 2 & up

Snails, like all slow, slimy critters, are irresistible to kids. Though some children may be apprehensive about touching slime, adventuresome kids will lead the way. Before long, kids will involve the snails in all sorts of zany play.

MATERIALS

Snails (the more the better)
Watercolor brushes
Moist washcloths or paper towels
Magnifying lenses
Green fleshy leaves, such as lettuce
Bug boxes
Plastic lids
Plant stems
Container with lid

The Setup

Place moist washcloths or paper towels on a table. Elicit ideas about how to handle snails with care. Set out other materials and the container of snails. To prevent snails from being hurt, monitor the play and intervene when snail lives are threatened.

The Science

How and why a snail retreats or emerges from its shell is among the many topics kids will question and investigate. Children may engage in beginning slimology and track snail movements. They may also undertake dietary studies.

Care & Feeding

Check with local gardeners to find out if any snails or slugs are available. Most likely they will be only too glad to get rid of them. Pick the leaves of the plants that they have been eating and place the leaves and snails in a container. Cover the container with a moist cloth secured with a rubber band. Keep in a cool dark place.

Real Life Science (ages 5–7)

"Oooh" was the initial response. Katelyn and Lea watched their snails from a safe distance. Nalani touched her snail and commented, "Yuck, I touched it."

After ten minutes, all the kids had touched their snails. Katelyn showed Lea how to pick up a snail by its shell. Nick placed a snail on his hand and turned his hand over. "It sticks. Look!"

The kids compared their snails.

"Look, mine is sticking to a leaf."

"Mine is climbing."

"Water is coming out of mine."

"Mine is one of those kind that always stays out."

"I saw mine come out of its shell."

"When I yell at mine, it comes off its leaf."

"When you push in his antennae, they grow back."

Questions popped out like emerging snail antennae.

"How does the head come out?"

"How come mine won't come out?" asked Rico as he prodded a snail with a brush.

"Do snails swim?" asked Ricky.

"What is this yellow stuff?"

"What is this black stuff coming out?" asked Amanda, "It looks like poop. It is!"

Despite or perhaps because of the slime and poop, snails were popular objects of playful study for many days.

Caterpillars

Caterpillars accompany most children home at some point in their childhood career. Whether it's their slowness or gentle behavior, kids welcome caterpillars like lost teddy bears. Kids will let them roam over their hands and up their arms. They will make them "homes" and use them in imaginative play. Through play, children will become aware of the unique behaviors and features of their new crawly friends.

Most caterpillars are perfectly safe, though a few uncommon species may protect themselves with irritating hairs. To avoid negative experiences with caterpillars, expose children to common caterpillars that you know are fail-safe (see below). By the time a child brings you a caterpillar on their own, you will most likely know if they have captured a chemically defensive caterpillar or not.

MATERIALS
Caterpillars (all the same kind)

Leaves from the plant they were found on

Watercolor brushes

Magnifying lenses

Bug boxes

The Setup

Place the materials at a table and elicit ideas about how to handle caterpillars with care. Ask who wants to play with a caterpillar and provide each of those kids with one. Some children may just want to watch the other kids first before they are ready for their own. Encourage kids who want more than one to share with other kids. Children can easily lose track of a caterpillar if they handle more than one at a time, and wandering caterpillars are in imminent danger of getting squished.

Where to Get

In most places, you can only find caterpillars in spring or summer. Look on trees, shrubs, or garden plants. If you or your kids collect your own, be sure to collect leaves from the plant they were found on and to remember where the plant was located. Many caterpillars, such as the tomato hornworm, which gardeners regard as a pest, are perfect for kids. Once alerted, local gardeners will happily award you with these unwanted munchers. Another source of caterpillars may be the local educational establishment. Many teachers maintain populations of silkworms from year to year. Silkworms need mulberry leaves for food. If you have a source for mulberry leaves, put out the word that you need silkworms. Fail-proof but more expensive sources of caterpillars are biological supply houses that sell popular caterpillars along with packaged food (see appendix).

Care & Feeding

Any large container with air holes will make a fine home for caterpillars. Supply them with fresh leaves every other day. Use only leaves from the kind of plant you found them feeding on. Caterpillars are picky eaters and will not eat just any leaves.

Cabbage butterflies only eat plants in the cabbage family while monarchs prefer milkweed. Keep the leaves fresh by wrapping their stems in a moist cloth or paper towel. Completely empty the container once a week to clean out the droppings that can become quite numerous when the caterpillars reach full size.

The Science

Caterpillars invite children to investigate feeding and defensive behaviors, as well as locomotion. Unlike many other animals, caterpillars provide the opportunity for children to witness the amazing process of metamorphosis.

Real Life Science (ages 5–7)

The kids excitedly welcomed their fuzzy guests, and soon the caterpillars were curled up in little palms or were traveling up arms.

"It tickles!" exclaimed Alex as he placed a caterpillar on his arm and then quickly transferred it back to his hand. "Now it's curled up," he continued. While Alex wondered how to get his critter uncurled, the rest of the children noticed other amazing things.

Claire peered through a magnifying lens and reported that her caterpillar was big and had lots of legs. Rico discovered that his caterpillar could hang onto a leaf and said "See, it sticks," as he displayed it to other kids.

"Oooh, he's pooping!" Emily cried out as she discovered the evidence on her arm. "I don't want you to poop anymore," she told the caterpillar. Later, she also discovered that the caterpillars made letters. "I'll call this one 'C' because it made a C and this one 'L' because it looks like an L."

Despite all the excitement, some kids just quietly played with their new fuzzy friends. Humberto silently watched his caterpillar climb out of a bug box and then placed a leaf in front of it. When it crawled onto the leaf, he turned it, watching how it continued to hold on. Matteo tore up leaves to make a caterpillar bed. Katelyn sat quietly holding and petting her new pal.

Rolypolies

ages 2 & up

With or without adult encouragement, kids have long collected rolypolies—or pill bugs—as pets and playmates. They are safe, active, easy-to-care-for critters, and are just right for kids' small fingers. If you provide tools and a place to explore, these little animals will further enrich kids' adventures with their rolypoly friends.

MATERIALS

Rolypolies (the more the better)
Watercolor brushes
Magnifying lenses
Large leaves
Plant stems
Tub of soil

The Setup

Ask for ideas about how to prevent rolypolies from getting hurt. Kids who still grasp things with strong pincer grasps may accidentally crush them. Encourage these children to pick up rolypolies with a stick or brush. Set up on an indoor or outdoor table. Provide children with cups or tubs to keep track of their rolypolies. Watch to make sure that none are ending up on the floor where they can be crushed by giant kid feet.

The Science

Children may be particularly attentive to the way rolypolies move and how they curl up in a ball. Rolypoly reactions to light and water may also be subjects of study. Other children may wonder what rolypolies eat and even investigate their food preferences.

Care & Feeding

Rolypolies are common residents of gardens and yards. Look for them under rocks, boards, or compost piles. In cold climates, they may be difficult to find in the winter. Rolypolies survive comfortably in a plastic tub if provided with a layer of moist soil covered with moist dead leaves. Feed them fruit scraps and keep the soil moist, not soggy.

Real Life Science (ages 2–5)

The rolypolies were a big hit at the preschool. Rhea was excited. "It's hiding. This is cool." Her rolypoly was crawling on a stem, and she predicted to Nathan, "It's on the stick and it is gonna fall off." Meanwhile, Nathan was peering through the lens looking at rainbows. Nearby, Nalani was carefully examining a rolypoly through the lens. She peered from different angles and distances.

Emmy and Nick were busy making a rolypoly house out of a tub and a plastic bag. Emily made a house with a yogurt container and an ivy leaf for the roof. She placed her rolypolies inside and covered them with dirt.

The kids made many great discoveries about the rolypolies, as well as homes for them. Nalani and Rhea found out they could pick up the pill bugs by placing a stick in front of them to climb aboard. Nick spied "eggs" on the underside of one rolypoly. As Emmy dropped bits of leaves into the tub, she asked the rolypolies, "Do you want to eat a leaf? Do you want to eat a stick? He's eating. They like sticks. They like leaves!"

Emmy carefully carried something over to Sean and placed it in his container. "I found one," she said. Emily peeked at it and exclaimed, "No, it's a rock. A rock is not a bug!"

Timmy, a two-year-old, unfortunately demolished several rolypolies. The first was squished as he pressed a magnifying lens on top of it to get a look. The second and third were smashed between his thumb and forefinger. I knew Timmy well and didn't think the killing was intentional. As I watched him hold other objects, I realized that he still used a pincher grasp and, unfortunately for the rolypolies, his grasp was quite strong. After realizing this, I asked Nalani to show Timmy how to pick up a rolypoly with a stick, and this seemed to work better.

On another day when we had the rolypolies set up at an outside table, all of the children abandoned the critters after about fifteen minutes, except two-year-old Sean. He stayed and played with the roly-polies for over fifty minutes, while the other children stopped by to see what he was doing.

Other Critters to Touch

Wherever you live, a wide variety of other harmless creatures are probably available for kid investigations. Below is a list of some of these animals and tips on how to host them. You can find information on others in the books listed in the bibliography on page 192. Be sure to make hand lenses available for all explorations.

Millipedes

These long, skinny, multi-legged critters are often confused with centipedes. Centipedes have a relatively flat body and possess only one pair of legs per body segment. They also have stingers. Millipedes on the other hand wear twice as many legs per segment and usually have a greater number of segments. They don't have stingers, and their bodies often have a rounder shape. Though millipedes don't sting, they can make a stink.

Care & Feeding

Found under logs and rocks during the day, millipedes cruise backyards, gardens, and sometimes even hallways in the dark hours. They are easy to keep for a couple of days in a tub of soil topped with a layer of moist leaves.

The Setup

Since millipedes are slow and have great traction, they are easy to examine on a table. Provide children with a small paintbrush and a jar lid with water.

Crickets & Grasshoppers

There are certain times of the year when children will bring crickets and grasshoppers home. You can lead children from collecting to observing by helping them set up a cricket or grasshopper observatory.

Care & Feeding

You can keep both crickets and grasshoppers in a terrarium or lidded tub. Line the bottom with soil and provide a snack of lettuce leaves. Before allowing children to handle these hoppers, show them how to hold one by its thorax or two back legs. Teaching yourself how to do first this may take some practice.

The Setup

Kids can observe these animals in the classroom in a large clear plastic bin. Since both crickets and grasshoppers have difficulty hopping on smooth surfaces such as linoleum or Formica tabletops, you can set up explorations on tables or floors. It's helpful to put these active insects on ice beforehand to slow them down.

Mealworms

These beetle grubs (also called white worms or golden grubs) are available at pet stores and are fascinating creatures to play with. Since they metamorphose into beetles, they provide a great opportunity for children to observe this amazing process.

Care & Feeding

As its name implies, the mealworm feeds on grain meals, such as cornmeal or wheat flour. Keep mealworms in a covered container—a shoebox works well. Cover the bottom of the box with a 1-inch layer of oatmeal, cornmeal, or flour. The grubs will extract water, as well as nutrition, from this meal. Extra water moisture can come from a slice of a carrot, a potato, or an apple. When the meal supply gets low or if you smell ammonia, transfer the grubs to a new box with a new layer of meal.

The Setup

Tabletop explorations are ideal for these safe, slow creatures. Though they lack the personality of more active creatures such as rolypolies, they will still be of interest to young children.

Ladybugs

Since ladybugs have a good reputation with kids, children will handle and collect them without fear. Gardeners are also fond of ladybugs because these beetles feed on small, plant-eating bugs called aphids.

Care & Handling

Providing fresh food for ladybugs can be a challenge because aphids—ladybugs' main meal—are found on live plants. Rather than keeping ladybugs as household guests, it works best to release them after kids have had an opportunity to investigate them. Though ladybugs may occasionally nip, their bite is harmless.

Cucumber Beetles

Children may discover these striped beetles on garden plants, where they munch leaves. In large numbers, they can become a gardener's nemesis. When you start collecting them and removing them from plants, neighborhood gardeners will appreciate it.

Care & Handling

Keep them inside a covered tub or terrarium. They are plant feeders, and prefer the leaves and flowers of bean, squash, corn, and pea plants. After picking the leaves, wrap the stems with a moist paper towel and bind them together with a rubber band. Change the leaves daily.

The Setup

Like ladybugs, these small beetles will crawl up arms and in and out of obstacle courses. Allow kids to place a variety of objects in a tub for the beetles to crawl on before you release the bugs for further observation.

Kid Science Library

Fiction

Carle, Eric. *The Grouchy Ladybug*. New York: Scholastic, 1977.

A ladybug challenges many creatures to fight. Have kids compare the ladybugs they observe in the exploration kit with the ladybugs in this book.

Carle, Eric. *The Very Hungry Caterpillar*. New York: Philomel, 1981.

A hungry caterpillar eats its way through everything—from apples to ice cream cones—on its way to butterflyhood. Read this after children have explored real caterpillars and have them compare fiction and reality.

Carle, Eric. *The Very Quiet Cricket*. New York: Philomel, 1990.

A young cricket finally gets to sing. Read before and after observing crickets.

Elhert, Lois. *Feathers for Lunch*. New York: Harcourt, 1990.

A house cat encounters twelve birds in the backyard, fails to catch any, and gets nothing but a feather for lunch. Read this before students examine a variety of feathers with magnifying lenses or microscopes.

Graham, Margaret Bloy. *Be Nice to Spiders*. New York: Harper and Row, 1967.

The zookeepers discover that spiders make life more comfortable for the zoo animals. Encourage kids to find old webs and examine them with hand lenses.

Heller, Ruth. *How to Hide a Butterfly and Other Insects*. New York: Grosset, 1986.

This and other books in Heller's Hide Series provide an interesting introduction to camouflage. Encourage students to make small camouflaged animals and hide them in the school yard.

Hines, Anna Grossnickle. *Remember the Butterflies*. New York: Dutton, 1991.

The story their grandfather once told them about a dead butterfly in the garden later helps some children understand his own death. Read this after the death of an animal.

Hoberman, Mary Ann. *A House is a House for Me*. New York: Viking, 1978.

Unforgettable rhymes playfully describe dwellings. Take the kids hunting for animal homes; set up blinds to watch animal burrows.

Howe, James. *I Wish I Were a Butterfly*. San Diego, CA: Harcourt, 1987.

A cricket wants to be a butterfly.

Leo, Lionni. *Inch by Inch*. New York: Astor Honor, 1960.

This story of an inchworm is a wonderful book to read after kids discover inchworms.

Martin, Bill Jr. *Polar Bear, Polar Bear. What Do You Hear?* New York: Scholastic, 1992.

Read this before taking a walk to listen to the sounds of local critters.

Mazer, Anne. *The Salamander Room*. New York: Knopf, 1991.

A boy finds a salamander in the woods and thinks of ways to make the perfect home for it. Read this book when children catch animals.

Marzollo, Jean. *Pretend You're a Cat*. New York: Dial, 1990.

A wonderful introduction to acting out animal behavior.

Parnall, Peter. *Feet!* New York: MacMillan, 1988.

A close-up examination of a variety of animal feet. This book is a great inspiration for examining the anatomy of different creatures.

Ryder, Joanne. *The Snail's Spell*. New York: Puffin, 1982.

A great book to follow snail investigations.

Selsam, Millicent E. *Terry and the Caterpillars*. Harper and Row, 1962.

Terry learns about the life cycle of moths when she keeps caterpillars in a jar.

Van Allsburg, Chris. *Two Bad Ants*. Boston: Houghton Mifflin, 1988.

Two ants have an early morning adventure during a human's breakfast. Read when kids are watching ants. Provide them with sugar and salt if they want to conduct feeding tests.

Weisner, David. *Tuesday*. New York: Clarion, 1991.

Read after children have had the opportunity to observe tadpoles and frogs.

Wildsmith, Brian and Rebecca. *Look Closer*. San Diego, CA: Harcourt, 1993.

An invitation to look closely for bugs.

White, E. B. *Charlotte's Web*. New York: Harper and Row, 1952.

This classic tale of a remarkable spider is full of spider natural history.

Wood, Audrey. *Quick as a Cricket*. New York: Childs Play, 1982.

A romp through an exciting array of animal attributes. This book will encourage children to act out animal behaviors.

Yoshi. *The Butterfly Hunt*. Boston: Picturebook Studio, 1993.

A little boy captures a large yellow butterfly and learns about freedom. Read before or after collecting bugs.

Nonfiction

Arnosky, Jim. *Crinkleroot's Book of Animal Tracking*. New York: Bradbury Press, 1989.

Use to track animals at school or home. Place flour or sand where you think animals might leave tracks.

Burnie, David. *Eyewitness Birds*. New York: Knopf, 1988.

A fact-filled introduction to birds.

Chatham, Clarence, and Herbert S. Zim. *Insects*. New York: Golden Press, 1987.

A picture-rich introduction to insects.

Dewey, Jennifer Owings. *Spiders Near and Far*. New York: Dutton, 1993.

A gallery of life-sized drawings of spiders.

Frichter, George S., and Herbert S. Zim. *Spiders and Their Kin*. New York: Golden Press, 1969.

A complete yet compact guide.

Eyewitness Junior Books about Animals. New York: Dorling Kindersly.

Informative series of books on birds, reptiles, butterflies, etc.

Glaser, Linda. *Wonderful Worms*. Brookfield, CT: Millbrook Press, 1992.

Accurate illustrations show earthworms in their habitat. Includes a "Facts About Wonderful Worms" spread.

Milne, Lorus and Margery. *Insects and Spiders*. New York: Doubleday, 1992.

A book of fundamental and fascinating facts about bugs.

Mitchell, Robert T., and Herbert S. Zim. *Butterflies and Moths*. New York: Golden Press, 1987.

A general introduction to these insects.

Parker, Nancy Winslow, and Joan Richards Wright. *Bugs*. New York: Morrow, 1987.

A compendium of bug lore.

Pigdon, Keith, and Marilyn Woolley. *Earthworms*.
Cleveland: Modern Curriculum Press, 1989.

This big book is terrific for browsing, as well as for
adult-aided research to find the answers to questions
that arise from inquiry.

Ross, Michael Elsohn. *Cricketology*. Minneapolis:
Carolrhoda Press, 1995.

A cricketologist's exploration manual.

Ross, Michael Elsohn. *Rolypolyology*. Minneapolis:
Carolrhoda Press, 1995.

A comprehensive guide to the study of rolypolies!

Ross, Michael Elsohn. *Snailology*. Minneapolis:
Carolrhoda Press, 1995.

A complete guide to slimy animal investigations.

Ross, Michael Elsohn. *Wormology*. Minneapolis:
Carolrhoda Press, 1995.

An entire book about the process of exploring
worms!

Smith, Hobart M., and Herbert S. Zim. *Reptiles and
Amphibians*. New York: Golden Press, 1987.

A guide full of facts and detailed art.

Kitchen Science

Eight

Preparing food is one of the most appreciated of sciences. It is an art based in an understanding of the palate, visual stimulus, chemical reactions, and physical possibilities. When children assist adults in cooking, they watch ingredients blending and interacting. They see concoctions froth and boil. They observe solids transforming to liquids and vice versa. It's mysterious and, better yet, delicious.

When we can begin to see preparing food as a science, it is easier to see the real value of letting kids join us in creating culinary masterpieces. When we see the cooking process as an opportunity for discovery, we can assist kids in creating truly unique—and sometimes inedible—dishes. Giving a child room to learn how to work safely in a kitchen may also be the best preparation for later experiences in a chemistry lab or an operating room. All cooks must learn a healthy respect for hot stoves, sharp knives, and other hazardous tools.

Children can learn to use small serrated knives at an early age. With close monitoring, grownups can prevent accidents. Knowing when a child is ready to respect a knife involves a detailed knowledge of a child's temperament. My son and his friends have helped me make salads and soups since they were three. I was careful to give them items that were easy to cut and to turn my attention toward them while they learned to slice. I doubt if my son received more scratches than me.

Meaty Discoveries

A kitchen that is a home to carnivores (meat eaters) is a laboratory where children can investigate animal anatomy. There are kidneys, hearts, and livers to examine and dissect. There are fat and muscles to experiment with. There are bones to study.

Welcome kids' participation in the preparation of the animals we eat. As they help, you can count on them asking about the various parts they encounter whether they are assisting in cleaning a fish or dressing a chicken. Playing the dual role of chef and surgeon can lead to some real tasty enlightenment.

Without adult supervision, kids' kitchen explorations can lead to disaster. If you find the appropriate time for exploration—though it may be a challenge—it will yield wonderful results. Choosing when to use kid assistants also takes some thought. Letting children prepare food for themselves is much different from having them prepare a banquet for your boss. Welcome to the kitchen lab. Bon appetit!

Plant Anatomy Explorations

Every time they prepare a plant part for consumption, apprentice cooks have the chance to learn a little more about the composition of plants. As children slice or tear apart the plants that we eat, they will make discoveries about different plant structures, textures, tastes, and colors. They will examine the plant "guts" and plant "skins." They will make comments and ask questions. As with other explorations, we need not be professional botanists to encourage inquiry. We merely need to consider what they are wondering about and add what we wonder, too.

Whether kids prepare the parts for soups, salads, or casseroles, they will develop a greater sense of plants. Give them freedom to choose how to slice a plant part, unless it is only safe to cut it a particular way.

Allow them to experiment with plant parts if they see the need. An interest in planting things can lead to burying everything from scallion roots to avocado seeds. A curiosity about rotten vegetables can take a child into the moldering realm of decomposition. Backyard compost piles, dead plant burials, or cleaning the refrigerator can develop a child's sense of decay.

Plant Prints

When kid artists use plant parts for stamps, they may embark upon mass art production. As they create repetitive patterns, they may point out to each other the unique shapes and textures of each different item used.

The Setup

Fill each pan with a different color paint to a depth of one-half inch. Slice the larger fruits and vegetables in half and place each slice in a pan. Allow them to soak for half an hour. When the slices are saturated with paint, take them out of the pans and place them on a tray or cookie sheet. Demonstrate how to press them on the paper to make a print, and let the kids go at it.

MATERIALS

Vegetables and fruits, such as onions, apples, zucchini, peppers, and radishes

3 to 4 baking pans

Newsprint or newspaper

Poster paint

Tray or cookie sheet

The Science

Each plant part has specific characteristics. For example, fruits are composed of a swollen ovarian wall and developed ovules, called seeds. Despite basic similarities, the plant world exhibits an incredible diversity of form and structure in all its individual species. Making plant prints can lead kids to comparing structures, shapes, and textures.

Real Life Science (ages 3–7)

Nissa silently examined the imprint made by each different plant part before she moved on to the next. After she used all the different ones, she printed a whole page of one type of plant part. With a grin of accomplishment, she surveyed the repetitive images. Beside her, Dana explored the patterns made by slicing off one end of a bell pepper. After she made each imprint, she looked at it and then peered inside the piece of pepper. Only the outside edge of the pepper left a print. On another day, Matteo also explored printing with peppers. After getting the same outline imprint, he smeared the inside of the pepper with paint. But, when he printed again, only the outline showed up.

As the children examined shapes, some used them to make composite pictures. Nick, for example, arranged different shapes until he had created a face.

Several children noticed the concentric patterns left by the onion half and the stars inside the apple imprints. Others noticed the texture of the squash skins. Some identified the fact that many of the prints were round.

Potions

The art of cooking can appear as an act of alchemy to non-cooks. Breads rise as if possessed by a growing force—which, actually, it is—liquids become solids, solids become liquids, and concoctions froth and bubble. Unlike alchemy, cooking is a real science based on years of trial and error by alternately disgruntled and satisfied cooks.

Given the OK, children will enthusiastically throw together concoctions. With little interference from adults, they will often concoct mixtures with no consideration for edibility. When you invite them to make up a recipe for a dinner and provide a set of ingredients, they may create a palatable meal. With an ear to their questions, you can help guide them on further explorations

Award kids with a variety of kitchen cupboard ingredients, and they will mix potions with great enthusiasm. Along with kids' imaginations, the concoctions may also bubble, froth and flow.

MATERIALS
Salad oil

Baking soda

Vinegar

Cornstarch

Salt

Dish or clothes detergent

Mixing spoons

Bowls or pans

The Setup

This is a classic kitchen or backyard activity, but can also work in a more institutional environment if set up as a small-group activity.

The Science

As kids create mixes, they may discover how some substances dissolve and others do not. When they mix vinegar and soda, they will encounter exciting chemical reactions. Pouring, stirring, and kneading goopy creations may also lead to discoveries about textures and solutions.

Real Life Science (ages 4–7)

As Nick sat at the picnic table, he pointed to the bottle of vinegar and said to Matteo and Timmy, "This is the stuff that does the stuff." Then he poured vinegar into a bowl of baking soda.

"It's going to overflow," Nick predicted.

"It's not going to overflow," countered Matteo.

Meanwhile, Timmy quietly measured out spoonfuls of different substances.

"Remember, we are not going to eat this." Mateo said to Nick, seeking reassurance that the awful-looking creation would never enter his mouth.

"Remember our plans," Nick replied. "We are pretending to make poison for the bad guys, I told you so. Look, it's overflowing."

Sure enough, Nick's potion was in full frothing action.

Matteo examined it closely and noticed "tunnels." Timmy's potion was now bubbling, and he leaned over it to listen to it fizz.

As more stuff was added, not only did the mixes change, but the imaginative play transformed as well. As the mixes thickened, the kids became cooks making dough. When it became gloppy, they were bears eating honey.

Kid Science Library

Fiction

de Paola, Tomie. *Pancakes for Breakfast*. New York: Harcourt, 1978.

This funny, wordless tale is about making pancakes from scratch, beginning with the cow. A good book to precede pancake making, what else?

de Paola, Tomie. *Strega Nona*. New York: Simon and Schuster, 1975.

Trouble ensues when a boy messes with a magic pot of pasta. Read this before exploring the cooking of dried foods.

Miller, J. P. *The Little Red Hen*. Racine, WI: Western, 1954.

Use this classic tale to introduce kids to bread making from scratch.

Root, Phyllis. *Soup For Supper*. New York: Harper and Row Publishers, 1986.

A fun introduction to making vegetable soup.

Wood, Audrey. *Heckedy Peg*. New York: Harcourt, 1981.

A story about food and magic.

Nonfiction

Cobb, Vicki. Science *Experiments You Can Eat*. New York: HarperCollins, 1972.

An introduction to the science of food preparation.

Outdoor Explorations

Nine

Excursions

You don't have to hike in the wilderness to journey through nature with a child. You don't have to go anywhere in particular or plan out exactly what you will see. Often, adults are blinded by goals and miss adventures as they unfold. Drawn to destinations, as if in a trance, they may ignore the way they came. Kids, on the other hand, get so involved in each step that getting to the end of the trail is sometimes quite a surprise. There are clouds to study, cracks to investigate, and bugs to follow. There's plenty to see everywhere.

Walking with children is a privilege, and we should do our best to let them lead the way. Once we accept the idea that our children may have the best notion of how to explore, we can concentrate on having an exciting and safe trip.

As caretakers, we can gently nudge them away from hazardous places such as highways, cliff tops, dumps, or groves of poison oak and nettle. We can alert them to dangers such as lightning, stinging centipedes, or broken glass. We can help them become aware of potential mishaps. However, we can also go overboard and frighten them so much that they'll never consider stepping out the front door again.

As outfitters, we can provide kids with exploration tools and comfortable attire. When kids begin to examine minutiae, we can pull magnifying lenses out of our pockets. When explorations go subterranean, we can hand over the trowels. When tadpoles need catching, we can help them scrounge nets.

Name Game

Have you ever shied away from taking children on an outdoor exploration because you didn't know the names of wild plants and animals? Did you ever consider that you don't need to know the name of something to look at and enjoy it? The process of investigating flora and fauna is more important than the process of naming it. Kids are not inhibited by not knowing the right names. Few children have ever heard the name terrestrial isopod, but that hasn't stopped them from dubbing bugs with names like rolypolies, potato bugs, and tiggle hogs. Nor has it prevented them from playfully exploring these fascinating animals. Kids naturally make up their own names for new things that they find, and we can too. When kids show an interest in learning the "real" names, we can give them field guides and encourage them to sift through the pictures.

Watchless Watch

To get in the right mood to explore outdoors with kids, you might want to leave your watch at home. Let your journeys be guided by curiosity, not schedules. Join in the wonder and go where it takes you!

Kindergardens

Whether the kid is Dennis the Menace or your own child, we often chide them for messing about in the garden. Amidst prize roses and award-winning tomatoes, it's sometimes hard to explore without getting in trouble. Even though gardens may be great places for producing food and floral extravaganzas, they are even better places for raising young scientists. Gardens can be snack bars, wildlife preserves, and discovery centers for uncovering the connections between living things. Without much effort, you can transform your backyard into a real kinder-garden.

Pest with a Pink Tail

Most gardeners respond to voracious critters like the tomato hornworm with a mixture of horror and indignation. How could it dare to munch half of a tomato? Who invited it to dinner?

While we were messing around in the garden one day, my son Nick, then two years old, discovered a humongous hornworm in the tomato plants. He stood eye level to the insect as it chomped on the foliage. Nick's sense of delight melted away my anxieties about the "pest." I stopped my weeding and stood by his side while he pointed out the exciting features of our garden guest. Though a brief examination sufficed for me, Nick continued to investigate after I had returned to my weeding. Had it been the size of an alligator, I would have most certainly have remained glued to the spot, but that didn't matter to Nick. In fact, the tiny size of this creature may have made it even more attractive to him.

When I discovered another hornworm, Nick scrutinized it closely and then returned to the first one. Back and forth he went between the hornworms comparing features. Then, taking me by the hand, he lead me to both and showed me that one had a pink tail horn and the other didn't. Together we pondered the mysteries of pink tails and, amazingly, I grew fond enough of the hornworms to feel disappointed when I discovered that they were missing a week later.

Garden Playground

A garden rich with diverse colors, textures, and smells is a jungle landscape to small children. Shrubs and tangled vines are secret hideouts. Fallow beds are places where kids can explore worms, roots, and rocks. Vegetables that are usually ignored at dinner are trailside snacks. Pests are pets.

You can create such a garden without greatly sacrificing vegetable production. Place important crops out of harm's way in raised planter boxes, which not only exclude little feet but gophers as well. Wide paths in high food production areas allow kids access without the danger of them running over plants. Other areas can be served by narrow serpentine paths well suited for exploring and hiding. Though perhaps lacking in the formal beauty of a well-manicured garden, a kid garden can be a more relaxing place. Since few parents or teachers of small children have the time to keep a tame garden, purposely cultivating a semi-wild patch can be a good excuse for taking the low maintenance path.

Snack Bar

You can fill a garden with snacks that require little preparation before consumption. Carrots merely need to be plucked and hosed off. Cucumbers, beans, and sugar snap peas can be munched right off the vine. Lettuce can be nibbled, and cherry tomatoes popped directly into the mouth.

Even when you serve it in the kitchen, homegrown produce is often better than the same stuff from the market. Somehow, the process of seeing it grow makes it less nasty.

A sense of ownership grows when kids have a choice in what they plant. Pick through the seed packs and plant crops that elicit a "yum yum."

Wildlife Garden

Flashy goldfinches and homely sparrows love sunflower seeds. Hummingbirds adore red sages and penstemons. Brilliant yellow butterflies arise from cabbage-munching caterpillars. Robins and other thrushes go crazy over pyracanthas and other berry-bearing shrubs. Warblers, flycatchers, and other bug-munching birds will inhabit your garden as long as you keep it free of toxic insecticides. The wildlife appeal of your garden is directly related to the plants that you raise and how you care for them. Are you ready to host a colorful menagerie in your backyard? Check out the list of gardening books on page 196 for sources of information on how to create a backyard wildlife sanctuary.

Sensory Garden

Kids are especially in tune with their senses, and a rich garden is a sensory feast. Fuzzy leaves. Whiffs of mint. Sniffs of basil. Mouthfuls of berries. Earfuls of bird and bug song. When choosing plants, consider their sensual properties. Herbs such as oregano, rosemary, and thyme are not only useful in cooking, but for cooking up images of food. The scents of lavender, mint, onion, and jasmine conjure up moods. Pussy willows, prickly roses, and lamb's quarters invite tactile explorations.

Though mostly pleasant, planting for the senses can sometimes be a tortuous experience. Did you know that there are flowers that smell like chocolate or leaves that conjure images of pizza?

Poisonous Plants

Some of our most common garden plants, such as oleander, calla lily, foxglove, and tomatoes, can prove dangerous if kids ingest the wrong parts. Whether you avoid growing these plants altogether or not, it's important to teach kids about the hazards of indiscriminately eating plants. Call your local poison control center if you have any doubts about the edibility of any plant that a child may have ingested.

Compost Gardens

ages 2 & up

Composting is an invitation to explore decomposition. Cooked by micro-organisms, the ingredients blend to make a topsoil casserole. Unlike the less obvious decay around us every day, the change in a compost pile is easier to monitor.

MATERIALS
Dried Leaves
Fruit and vegetable scraps
Planting pots
Potting soil
Watering can

The Setup

To make a safe, innocuous compost pile, you need to follow some basic rules. Since meat and dairy products will attract skunks, rats, and snakes, leave them out. Avoid obnoxious odors by aerating the pile and making sure there is an equal balance of wet and dry materials.

There are many books that explain composting in detail; however, you can make a simple pile of alternating layers of dry materials, such as dried leaves or grass, and wet materials, such as kitchen scraps or manure. Occasionally add a thin layer of soil between layers to provide the micro-organisms needed for decay. Add a little water to supply the micro-organisms with the moisture they need. A pile that is as moist as a squeezed-out sponge is just perfect. It's not too wet or too dry. A pile the size of a washing machine is big enough for optimal decay, but not too big to turn. Whether you build piles in or out of a bin, it's helpful to put them in a spot where they won't get in the way. The total process of decay can take as long as three or four months, depending on your climate.

Each time you add materials to the pile, turn it, or use some for fertilizer. Invite kids to explore, and you will discover that it's a treasure of little creatures and interesting textures and aromas. Though kids may get messy, there are no health hazards to worry about.

Fruit and vegetable kitchen scraps can be a tremendous bonanza for the young plant propagator. Let kids experiment with everything from pineapple tops and scallion roots to apple cores and orange peels. Help them label and date each container that they plant in.

The Science

Compost piles are places where kids can study the process of decomposition in action. Compost is full of decomposers. Earth worms, isopods, beetles, and molds are easy to find. As apple cores, banana peels, and potato peels transform into humus, kids will see for themselves where topsoil comes from.

Real Life Science

Our home compost pile is a great place to carry on a bug search. My son and his friends often investigate the pile for worms or rolypolies. "What's that?" His friend Alex asked a dozen times as he helped turn the pile. There were beetles, sunflower sprouts, growing onion tops, and a bunch of other strange things to explore.

Mrs. Bown's class made a simple pile at school by simply dumping fruit and vegetable scraps in a hole in the garden. The hole was covered by soil and added to every once in a while. One day two girls returned from recess shouting. "It's growing, it's growing." The whole class ventured out to witness the miracle. Indeed, some potatoes that had been added to the compost were now sprouting from the pile.

Digging

Adults may need to use gardening as a pretense for messing around in the dirt, but kids merely need permission to dig. Once they get started, kids will excavate for hours. In the process, they might explore animal burrows, sift through soil particles, trace root paths, or pretend they are digging to the other side of the globe. Without a doubt, investigating the skin of Earth is a mission of childhood and adults should have the good sense to step aside and let kid geologists do their thing!

MATERIALS
Food containers of various sizes
Cookie cutters and molds
Kitchen strainers
Trowels or small sand shovels
Spoons or forks

The Setup

Set aside an area in part of your garden, backyard, or schoolyard where children can dig without getting into trouble. This could be a fallow bed, a designated dig site, or just an unused corner.

The Science

Soil is more than a substance; it is a rich ecosystem of interacting plants and animals. As children play with soil, they accumulate more than the obvious dirt on their hands and clothes. Poking around in the earth uncovers questions and experiences that lead to a greater understanding of the complexity of the ground beneath our feet.

Real Life Science (ages 5–7)

"Hey, this isn't a rock!" Rhyen exclaimed as he broke a dirt clod.

"It has rock in it," countered Pearl.

"Yeah, here's rocks," said Rhyen, holding up some pebbles in his palm. An earthen mound grew next to Rhyen and Pearl as they dug deeper. Pearl poked a hole in the top of the mound and said, "This is a crater."

"It's a volcano, but it's a crater, too," replied Rhyen.

Pearl had recently moved from a community on the other side of the mountains that is close to a series of volcanic craters. Rhyen had just been there on a school field trip, and he also had volcanoes on his mind.

As Pearl poured water into the crater hole, she said, "This is a stew of boiling lava. I made lava stew."

As Timmy dug, he was conscious that there were things to find. He said to Kyle, "If you dig real deep, you'll find worms."

After excavating for a minute, he announced, "I found a grasshopper leg."

Kyle examined the "leg" and disagreed. "No, it isn't," he said, "it's a stick!"

As Krista and Dana dug in some dry dusty soil, they discovered a gaping gopher hole. Krista declared that the hole itched and continued to excavate.

Children often spent recess exploring the soil in a fallow section of the school garden. For several days, one group unearthed the interlinking tunnels of resident gophers with the care of a team of archaeologists. On another occasion, some kids pretended to mine and washed off their "gem" discoveries in the drinking fountain. Sifting led to discoveries of roots that several children called "hair" and "special" rocks. And, of course, when we added water to the scene, dirt piles transformed into dirt soup, mud pies, or hot chocolate.

Seeds

A pile of seeds is something children seldom get to play with. Add tweezers, scales, and other instruments of exploration, and you'll witness some playful examinations of size, shape, and texture.

MATERIALS
One to 2 gallons of seeds
Magnifying lenses
Tweezers
Small plastic containers with lids
Funnels
Balance scales
Tubs
Acrylic tubing (1-inch diameter or bigger, 1- to 3-foot lengths)

The Setup

Make a mixture of seeds using several kinds of birdseed mix, rice, beans, spice seeds (such as dill and cumin), seeds from outdoor plants, and popcorn. The more variety the better. It's best to set up this kit outside in tubs, water table, or rigid plastic pool. Seeds spilled outdoors can become bird food. You can also set this up inside if you put it in an area where you can easily clean up the seeds.

Before letting the kids play, let them know that the seeds they will use are not clean enough to eat. Perhaps you can follow up the play with some edible seed snacks.

The Science

Playing with seeds exposes kids to the diversity of seeds and leads them to compare their characteristics. Kids can sort seeds by size, color, shape, or texture. Kids will explore volume and weight with the containers and scales. They will explore shape and movement with the tubing.

Real Life Science (ages 5–7)

The kids immediately began to put seeds in containers, pick them up with tweezers, and feel them with their fingers. They poured seeds through funnels into containers. They poured seeds into the balance scales. Seeds flowed from one container to another.

"Look, it's balancing," Allison said to Katelyn as she pointed at a scale.

Rico plugged the end of a funnel with a bottle cap and created an instant-release mechanism. "Watch," he said to Maira as he released seeds into her tub. Without delay, Maira made one for herself.

Amanda found an acrylic tube and, within a few minutes, four kids were arranged around the tube—supporting it, filling it with seeds, and directing the flow. Nick discovered that he could use an acorn as a plug.

Ali brought Amanda seeds, and Lea supplied Ali. Poured seeds flowed nonstop, like silo's feeding grain cars, until an acorn plugged the works. It became disengaged after the troubleshooters figured out that gently shaking the tube released it. Later, Nick and Amanda plugged both ends of the tube so that it was full of seeds and then used it to play tug of war.

Some of the kids who had been playing with ramps on the other side of the room came over to join in. Amanda and Nick went over to the ramps with their tube and a cup. Soon, seeds where flowing down the ramp. Making sounds like heavy machinery, Rickey and Rhyen poured seeds through funnels. Maira and Rico ran seeds through a contraption made of four funnels. Even during cleanup, the children continued to delight in pouring seeds.

Kid Science Library

Aardema, Verna. *Bringing the Rain to Kapiti Plain*. New York: Dial, 1981.

Animals live through a drought on an African plain. Experiment to see the effects of artificial drought on plants.

Anderson, Lena and Christina Bjork. *Linnea's Windowsill Garden*. New York: Farrar, Straus, and Giroux, 1988.

Linnea takes readers on a tour of her indoor garden and shares her skill at caring for plants.

Carle, Eric. *The Tiny Seed*. Boston: Picture Book Studio, 1987.

Read this after kids have played with seeds. Provide soil, containers, and seeds for planting.

Carlson, Nancy. *Harriet and the Garden*. Minneapolis: Carolrhoda Books, 1982.

A good book for dealing with the issue of trampling in a garden.

Carlstrom, Nancy White. *Wild, Wild Sunflower Child Anna*. New York: Alladin Books, 1987.

Read this book before planting sunflowers.

Coats, Laura Jane. *The Oak Tree*. New York: MacMillan, 1987.

Plant acorns or other tree seeds. Record the day you planted and monitor the trees' growth.

Cooney, Barbara. *Miss Rumphius*. New York: Puffin Books, 1982.

A woman plants lupine to make the world more beautiful. Read this before planting flowers.

de Paola, Tomie. *The Legend of Indian Paintbrush*. New York: Putnam and Sons, 1988.

Little Gopher follows his destiny and becomes an artist. Observe and paint sunsets, and compare them with the colors of flowers.

Dunrea, Olivier. *Deep Down Underground*. New York: MacMillan, 1989.

This counting book explores soil animals. Read this after children have dug in the soil. It may lead to more inquiry about soil animals.

Elhert, Lois. *Planting a Rainbow*. San Diego: Harcourt, Brace, Jovanovich, 1988.

How to grow a rainbow garden. Look through seed catalogs for pictures of plants from the book, order the seeds, and grow a garden with the kids.

Himmelman, John. *Amanda and the Magic Garden*. New York: Viking, 1987.

Amazing things happen in Amanda's garden.

Kaufman, Bob. *Watch My Tracks*. New York: Knopf, 1971.

Great for motivating kids to look for tracks outdoors.

Krauss, Ruth. *Carrot Seed*. New York: Harper and Row, 1945.

A boy plants a carrot seed, and it grows despite everyone else's predictions. Let kids plant carrot seeds.

Parnall, Peter. *Quiet*. New York: Morrow Junior Books, 1989.

A boy lies quietly and watches and listens to the world around him. After reading the book, take children outside to listen for sounds and to watch for animals or changes in the sky.

Potter, Beatrix. *The Tale of Peter Rabbit*. New York: Random, 1990.

Use this classic tale to stimulate investigations of the food habits of animals, particularly those in the garden.

Romanova, Natalia. *Once There Was a Tree*. New York: Dial, 1983.

A Russian tale about a decomposing tree. Explore a dead tree or other organism in the state of decay. Bury organic (apple cores or orange peels) and inorganic (plastic or metal) waste outside. Mark the spot, dig up the items after a month, and examine them for changes.

Ross, Michael. *Faces in All Kinds of Places*. El Portal, CA: Yosemite Association, 1986.

A worm explores the flowers growing on its rooftop. Go on a flower shape hunt. Search for flower visitors.

Soya, Kiyoshi. *A House of Leaves*. New York: Philomel, 1986.

Collect and explore a variety of leaves.

Titherington, Jeanne. *Pumpkin, Pumpkin*. New York: Greenwillow, 1986.

A young boy plants a pumpkin seed, watches it grow, picks it, and carves it into a jack-o'-lantern. He saves six seeds for planting. Plant some pumpkin seeds and watch them grow.

Tolstoy, Alexei. Illustrated by Helen Oxenberry. *The Great Big Enormous Turnip*. London: William Heineman, 1968.

Read this before letting kids pull out weeds and explore roots.

Ward, Leila. *I Am Eyes. Ni Macho*. New York: Scholastic, 1978.

A Swahili child observes the world around her.

Williams, Vera B. *Cherries and Cherry Pits*. New York: Greenwillow, 1986

A young girl's story about cherries and cherry pits. Allow kids to collect and plant a variety of seeds from fruits.

Parting Words Ten

In the three years that

I have been working on this book I have shared experiences with many parents, teachers, and kids. I have watched quiet little two-year-old scientists mature into babbling five-year-old masters. I have witnessed young teams of explorers becoming more and more adept at working together.

I have never ceased to be impressed by the skills, enthusiasm, and creativity of these wonderful younger folks. This book is a testimony to those marvelous encounters, and I hope it will encourage readers to embark on similar journeys. Please let me know of your experiences, ideas, and questions so that this book can become even more useful.

Appendix
Where to Get Supplies and Tools

Hardware Stores
A wide variety of tools and equipment are available at your local hardware store. Check at your local store for acrylic tubing, PVC pipe, funnels, pulleys, measuring tapes, pipe insulation, screwdrivers, pliers, plungers, and trowels.

Discards
There are many materials and tools that are also free for the asking. Ask lock and key shops for discarded locks and keys. Hospitals and clinics are a great source of plastic tubs, tubing, tweezers, and bottles with droppers. Construction sites yield discarded plastic pipes, gutters, and pipe insulation. Tile shops have leftover pieces of unglazed tiles, which are useful for rock explorations.

Making Explorer Tools

Pulley Board

MATERIALS

Two pulleys (with a 1-inch wheel)

Two eyehooks

Two 1-inch S hooks

Two 10-foot lengths of venetian blind cord

Lumber: 1x8, 20 inces long; 2x4, 4 feet long

Fence

TOOLS

Sander

Drill

HOW TO MAKE

1. After sanding the 1x8, drill two holes 2 inches from the end of either side of the board and 6 inches apart.

2. Loop the end of each cord through the end of the board and tie it to itself 6 inches above the board.

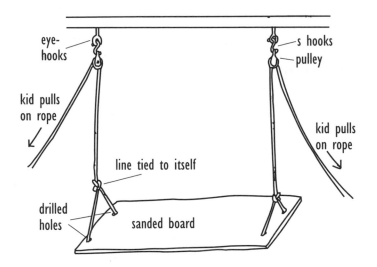

3. Set two eyescrews 16 inches from either end of the 2x4.

4. Drill ⅝-inch holes 1 inch from either end of the 2x4.

5. Place the 2x4, with eyescrews facing down, across the corner of the fence. Secure with cord.

6. Use the S hooks to attach the pulleys to the top eyescrews.

7. Thread each cord through a pulley on the 2x4.

Monochord

MATERIALS
36-inch piece of 1x2
Two eyescrews
Nylon fish line
Small wooden block

HOW TO MAKE

1. Set the eyescrews on either end of the board.

2. Tightly attach the fishing line between the screws.

3. Place the block under the nylon cord and it's ready to play with.

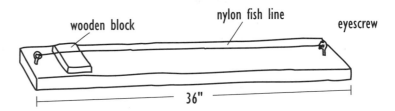

wooden block   nylon fish line   eyescrew

36"

Cardboard Guitars

MATERIALS

A cigar box or any similar sized box

Rubberbands of various thicknesses and lengths

Ruler

HOW TO MAKE

1. Place the rubber bands around the box in sequence from the thickest to narrowest. Set them apart at an equal distance.

2. Slide the ruler under the rubber bands to make a bridge which can be slid back and forth. Slide it close to one side.

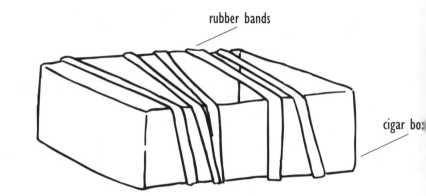

rubber bands

cigar box

PVC Pipe Stands

MATERIALS FOR EACH

Three 3-foot lengths of ½-inch PVC pipe

Four one-foot lengths of ½-inch PVC pipe

Two ½-inch PVC T fittings

Two ½-inch PVC right angle fittings

PVC pipe glue

HOW TO MAKE

1. Join a 1-foot length of pipe to either end of each T fitting and place 3-foot length in the upright hole.

2. Attach a right angle fitting to the other end of each of the 3-foot lengths.

3. Between the two upright pipes insert the other 3-foot pipe.

4. This stand can now be glued together one section at a time. Allow 24 hours of drying time before using.

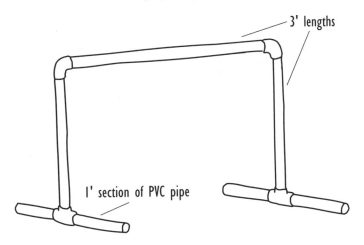

3' lengths

1' section of PVC pipe

Parachutes

MATERIALS FOR EACH
12-inch square of cloth
12-inch lengths of string
Large paper clip

HOW TO MAKE

Tie the end of each string to one corner of cloth. Tie the other ends togther. Attach the paper clip to the tie together strings.

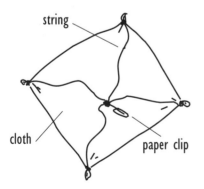

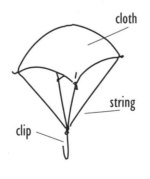

Whirlybirds

MATERIALS FOR EACH
One 9 x 3 piece of construction paper
One large paper clip

HOW TO MAKE

1. Make a 6-inch longitudnal cut up the middle of the paper

2. Fold the flaps at right angles in opposite directions.

3. Attach a paper clip at the middle of the uncut end and it's ready to whirl.

Giant Bubble Makers

MATERIALS FOR EACH

30 inches of venetian blind cord

Two 12-inch lengths of ¼- or ½-inch dowel

Two eyescrews

Five ¼-inch washers

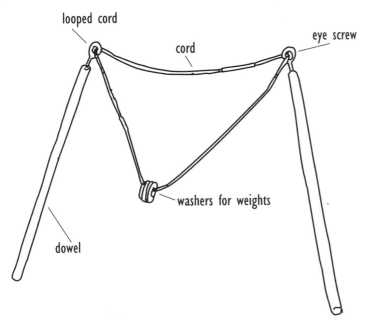

looped cord

cord

eye screw

washers for weights

dowel

HOW TO MAKE

1. Attach one eyescrew in one end of each dowel.

2. Thread the washers onto the cord and loop the ends of the cords through the eyescrews.

3. Tie the tow ends of the string together and hold the two dowels taut with the washers hanging down.

4. The string merely needs to be dipped into the bubble mixture to draw out large bubbles. Monitor them occasionally to make sure they aren't becoming tangled.

Pinwheels

MATERIALS FOR EACH
6-inch square of construction paper

Straw

Straight pin

Modeling clay

HOW TO MAKE

1. Draw diagonal lines from opposite corners of the paper and mark where they cross.

2. Cut each line from the corner to within one inch of the center.

3. Bend the left corner of one section toward the center, so that the tip overlaps. Bend each adjacent section until all the left corner tips overlap at the center.

4. Secure the center and all the tips by piercing with a pin. Poke the pin with attached pinwheel one inch from an end of the straw.

5. Place clay over the sharp protruding pin point and adjust the position of the pin until the wheel moves freely.

Air Wands

MATERIALS FOR EACH

3-foot length of ¼-inch dowel

Colored duct or electrical tape

Four 2-foot lengths of ribbon

HOW TO MAKE

Staple the ends of the ribbons together and attach them with tape to one end of the dowel.

Cone Timers

MATERIALS FOR EACH

Cone-shaped cup

Two clear plastic jars or cups of the same size

One cup of fine sand or salt

HOW TO MAKE

Make a very small hole in the tip of the cone cup with a pin or scissors. Show kids how to pour sand into the timer and how to start it over by placing the empty cone on the other cup.

Children's Literature and Science
A Bibliography

Annotated List of Resource Books for Parents and Teachers

Early Childhood Education

Devries, Rheta and Lawrence Kohlberg. *Constructivist Early Education: Overview and Comparison with Other Programs*. Washington, DC: National Association for the Education of Young Children, 1988.

A thick and thorough overview of theory and practice.

Rogers, Cosby S. and Janet K. Sawyers. *Play in the Lives of Children*. Washington, DC: National Association for the Education of Young Children, 1987.

Whether you need to justify play or want to understand it better this is the book for you. This concise overview of play is well documented by a fifteen-page reference list.

Van Horn, Judith. *Play at the Center of the Curriculum*. New York: MacMillan, 1993.

A guide to making play the focus of early childhood curriculum. Includes a wonderful section about the visit of scientists to a kindergarten class and their amazement at the science processes they see kids engaged in.

Early Childhood Science

Britain, Lory and Christine Chaille. *The Young Child as Scientist*. New York: HarperCollins, 1991.

Written primarily as a college text, this academic introduction to constructionist science is full of wonderful anecdotes and practical ideas for the classroom.

Hill, Dorothy M. *Mud, Sand, and Water.* Washington, DC: National Association for the Education of Young Children, 1977.

Illustrated with black-and-white photos, this slim book is a wonderful treatise on the importance of playing with mud, sand, and water.

Holt, Bess-Gene. *Science With Young Children.* Washington, DC: National Association for the Education of Young Children, 1989.

A comprehensive academic resource for teachers of young children. Philosophy is backed up by research and personal anecdotes.

Kohl, Maryann and Jean Potter. *Science Arts.* Bellingham, WA: Bright Ring, 1993.

A rich collection of art projects that lead to science explorations.

McIntyre, Margaret. *Early Childhood and Science.* Washington, DC: National Science Teachers Association, 1984.

A collection of practical articles from the journal *Science and Children.*

Nickelsburg, Janet. *Nature Activities for Early Childhood.* Phillipines: Addison-Wesley, 1976.

A great resource book for setting up nature activities.

General Science:

Criswell, Susie Gwen. *Nature Through Science and Art.* Blue Ridge Summit, PA: TAB, 1994.

A variety of directed activities that introduce science concepts through art.

Hampton, H. Carolyn. *Classroom Creature Culture.* Washington, DC: National Science Teachers Association, 1986.

This is a great collection of articles about the care and study of creatures in the classroom.

Stangl, Jean. *Science Toolbox.* Blue Ridge Summit, PA: TAB, 1994.

Tips on making simple science tools such as kites, flags, wind socks, wind chimes, magnets, prisms, stethoscopes, and many others.

Gardening:

Bradley, Fern Marshall and Barbara W. Ellis. *The Organic Gardener's Handbook of Natural Insect and Disease Control.* Emmaus, PA: Rodale Press, 1992.

An easy-to-use encyclopedia with complete instructions on how to safely protect your garden.

Campbell, Stu. *Let it Rot!* Pwnal, VT: Storey Publications, 1990.

A gardener's guide to composting.

Carlson, Laurie. *Green Thumbs: A Kid's Activity Guide to Indoor and Outdoor Gardening.* Chicago: Chicago Review Press, 1995.

With a few seeds, some water and soil, and this book, kids will be creating gardens of their own in no time.

Druse, Ken. *The Natural Garden.* New York: Clarkson Potter, 1988.

Learn how to design a garden that works with rather than against natural processes.

Ernst, Ruth Shaw. *The Naturalist's Garden.* Old Saybrook, CN: Globe Pequot Press, 1993.

A guide to designing a garden that attracts, houses, and shelters wildlife.

Gershuney, Grace and Deborah Martin. *The Rodale Book of Composting.* Emmaus, PA. Rodale Press, 1992.

An essential guide to composting with useful advice for apartment dwellers, as well as suburbanites. Includes plans for building compost bins.

Ocone, Lynn. *The Youth Gardening Book.* Burlington, VT: Gardens for All, 1983.

A guide to gardening with groups of kids, includes 28 activities and experiments.

Perenyi, Constance. *Growing Wild.* Hillsboro, OR: Beyond Words, 1991.

The story of a yard that goes "to seed" and transforms into a wildlife preserve.

Pyle, Robert Michael. *Handbook For Butterfly Watchers.* Boston: Houghton Mifflin, 1992.

Covers butterfly garden, rearing, identification, and ecology.

Tekulsky, Matthew. *The Butterfly Garden*. Cambridge, MA: Harvard Common Press, 1985.

A complete manual on how to attract this elusive animal to your garden.

Tilger, Linda. *Let's Grow: 72 Gardening Adventures with Children*. Pwnal, VT: Garden Way, 1985.

This book is full activities, projects, and exuberance.

Verey, Rosemary. *The Scented Garden*. New York: Random House, 1989.

How to choose, grow, and use fragrant plants.

Other Kids' Activity Books from Chicago Review Press

Big Book of Fun
Creative Learning Activities for Home & School, Ages 4–12
Carolyn Buhai Haas
Illustrated by Janet Bennet Phillips
Includes more than 200 projects and activities—from indoor-outdoor games and nature crafts to holiday ideas, cooking fun, and more.
ISBN 1-55652-020-4, 280 pages, paper, $11.95

Frank Lloyd Wright for Kids
Kathleen Thorne-Thomsen
A thorough biography is followed by stimulating projects that enable kids to grasp the ideas underlying Wright's work—and have fun in the process.
ISBN 1-55652-207-X, 144 pages, paper, $14.95

Green Thumbs
A Kid's Activity Guide to Indoor and Outdoor Gardening
Laurie Carlson
With a few seeds, some water and soil, and this book, kids will be creating gardens of their own in no time. They will also create compost, make watering cans, grow crazy cucumbers, and much more. Ages 3–9. ISBN 1-55652-238-X, 144 pages, paper, $12.95

Happy Birthday, Grandma Moses
Activities for Special Days Throughout the Year
Clare Bonfanti Braham and Maria Bonfanti Esche
Illustrated by Mary Jones
Two hundred related activities pay charming, educational tribute to the holidays, history, and accomplishments of many cultures and many people. Ages 3–9. ISBN 1-55652-226-6, 304 pages, paper, $14.95

Huzzah Means Hurray
Activities from the Days of Damsels, Jesters, and Blackbirds in a Pie
Laurie Carlson
Kids can re-create a long-ago world of kings, castles, jousts, jesters, magic fairies, and Robin Hood—all they need are their imaginations and materials they can find at home. Ages 3–9. ISBN 1-55652-227-4, 184 pages, paper, $12.95

Kids Camp!
Activities for the Backyard or Wilderness
Laurie Carlson and Judith Dammel
Fun and educational camping activities teach kids how to construct a tarp tent, make jean daypacks, tie knots, and even make the ultimate lunch: hot dogs and s'mores cooked in a solar oven. Ages 4–12. ISBN 1-55652-237-1, 184 pages, paper, $12.95

Look at Me
Creative Learning Activities for Babies and Toddlers
Carolyn Buhai Haas
Illustrated by Jane Bennet Phillips
Activities for babies and toddlers that inspire creativity and learning through play. ISBN 1-55652-021-2, 228 pages, paper, $11.95

Messy Activities and More
Virginia K. Morin
Illustrated by David Sokoloff
Foreword by Ann M. Jernberg
Encourages adults and children to have fun making a mess with more than 160 interactive games and projects.
Ages 3–10. ISBN 1-55652-173-1, 144 pages, paper, $9.95

More Than Moccasins
A Kid's Activity Guide to Traditional North American Indian Life
Laurie Carlson
Kids will discover traditions and skills handed down from the people who first settled this continent, including how to make useful pottery and communicate through Navajo code talkers. Ages 3–9. ISBN 1-55656-213-4, 200 pages, paper, $12.95

My Own Fun
Creative Learning Activities for Home and School
Carolyn Buhai Haas and Anita Cross Friedman
More than 160 creative learning projects and activities for elementary-school children.
Ages 7–12. ISBN 1-55652-093-X, 194 pages, paper, $9.95

These books are available through your local bookstore or directly from Independent Publishers Group, 814 N. Franklin Street, Chicago, Illinois 60610, 1-800-888-4741.
Visa and MasterCard accepted.